This book is the ultimate reality check, packed with practical advice and tips for undergoing a complete personal inventory. Learn to honestly access where you are, rediscover yourself, and transform into the person God designed you to be.

—Lindsey Simmons, publicity, social and digital media manager at Franciscan Media

Anthony Buono has written a wonderful blueprint on becoming a good Christian marriage candidate. This book is the result of his many years of encouraging hundreds of young Catholic men and women in their journey of dating and marriage and helping them to find each other online at www.AveMariaSingles.com.

So many writers on dating and courtship focus on what to look for in a potential spouse. Buono helps his readers look at themselves, to see if *they* are the kind of person who is prepared to be successful in marriage.

He presents virtue after virtue that every Christian should cultivate to become the person God wants them to be. His material is solidly Catholic, the kind of thing St. Francis de Sales might have written for someone hoping to marry well.

Would You Date You? is a recipe for holiness. Nothing could prepare a person better than this for a healthy, lasting marriage—and, of course, for the eternal marriage with God.

—Rev. T.G. Morrow, author of *Christian Courtship in an Oversexed World*

WOULD YOU DATE YOU?

WOULD YOU DATE YOU?

ANTHONY BUONO

Founder of Ave Maria Singles

SERVANT
BOOKS

PUBLISHED BY FRANCISCAN MEDIA
Cincinnati, Ohio

Unless otherwise noted, Scripture passages have been taken from the *Revised Standard Version*, Catholic edition. Copyright 1946, 1952, 1971 by the Division of Christian Education of the National Council of Churches of Christ in the USA. Used by permission. All rights reserved.

Cover and book design by Mark Sullivan

LIBRARY OF CONGRESS CATALOGING-IN-PUBLICATION DATA
Buono, Anthony M.
Would you date you? / Anthony Buono.
p. cm.
ISBN 978-1-61636-430-4 (alk. paper)
1. Single people—Religious life. 2. Christian life—Catholic authors. I. Title.
BX2373.S55B86 2012
248.8'4—dc23

2012016557

ISBN 978-1-61636-430-4

Published by Servant Books, an imprint of
Franciscan Media
28 W. Liberty St.
Cincinnati, OH 45202
www.FranciscanMedia.org
www.ServantBooks.org

Printed in the United States of America
Printed on acid-free paper
12 13 14 15 16   5 4 3 2 1

I dedicate this book to my seven beautiful children:
Mary, Isaac, Paul, Gregory, Lydia, Joseph, and Bethany.
May you keep becoming the people God intends
and inspires you to be.

CONTENTS

FOREWORD

WHEN ORIGINALLY ASKED TO WRITE a foreword for Anthony Buono's new book, *Would You Date You?*, I am told I was happy to do it. I don't recall that feeling, but Anthony tells me it's true and he knows best.

I've trusted Anthony as my personal dating coach for the past three years on my radio show: *The Catholic Guy* on SiriusXM's *The Catholic Channel*. And after several years of coaching me, just look at the results: I'm forty years old and still single.

Bravo, Anthony. Well done, good and faithful servant.

The truth is, it's not Anthony's fault. A single Catholic like me is Anthony's worst nightmare because I break all of his rules on dating, such as…

I like women to ask me out. Some say that's because I'm insecure and have a fear of rejection. But what does my therapist know?

I kiss on a first date. This horrifies Anthony. He worries about my chastity, and my eternal soul, but I also think he just doesn't like the visual. He writes a chapter on purity, and specifically kissing, which is worth the price of this book alone. Where else will you find a sentence like "But let us stay with closed-mouth kissing for a moment." Read on!

I don't pray on my dates as much as Anthony would like me to. Although I'm sure the women at times find themselves in prayer. Prayers like "Lord, when will this date end?"

But Anthony's persistent. He's patient. And he doesn't give up on anyone. Even cases like mine, which even St. Jude might quit on....

I disagree with about half the stuff Anthony tells me about dating. Not because Anthony is wrong. But because if I acknowledge how right he is...I'd have to change a lot of things in my life.

This would make me a better Catholic, and undoubtedly a better future spouse, but then I'd have to admit I don't have it all figured out. And none of us like admitting such things, do we?

You know, Anthony could have taken the easy way out and just given tips for dating: Look for this quality in a mate, avoid that quality in a mate, put your life in God's hands, and you'll live happily ever after!

Unfortunately, this book isn't filled with insights like why women date bad boys, why men are afraid to commit, and what's the best way to escape from a restaurant's bathroom window when a date isn't going well.

Instead, he forces us to look in the mirror and realize one reason we may be single is staring back at us. And we may not like what we see.

I love the name of this book. The question "Would you date you?" is a tough one to answer.

After thinking more about the question, however, my answer is yes. Though I'm not typically attracted to men with large noses, I'd be willing to date me. We have a lot in common, me and me.

So, yes, I'd date me. There, I said it. Then again, I'm reminded of the great Groucho Marx line, "I'd never want to be a member of any club that would have someone like me as a member."

But as Anthony likes to point out to me, perhaps the number one reason that I'm single is that I can't find anyone as messed up as me who would actually be crazy enough to date me. (It seems I must both improve myself... *and* find a woman who will be let out of the loony bin long enough for me to take her out on a date.)

But here are some things I know about Anthony Buono: He wants to help single people. He has a heart for single people. And he wants us all to find our love...while keeping our eyes on our truest love: God.

It's a topic everyone loves: love. And if this book doesn't help you find a spouse, it will at least help you to be a better Christian.

Actually, I don't know if that's true or not. I didn't get a chance to read the whole book, as I've been out promoting my own book *Sinner: The Catholic Guy's Funny, Feeble Attempts to Be a Faithful Catholic* (available at amazon.com or wherever fine books are sold).

But Anthony tells me this book is excellent. And he knows best. Did I mention he's been my dating coach the past three years and I'm still single?

—*Lino Rulli*

PREFACE

WHEN YOU'VE WORKED WITH SINGLES as long as I have, you inevitably deal with the same kinds of questions or concerns. "Why didn't he call after our first date?" "Why won't she just tell me what she's upset about?" "Why are men so picky?" "Why do women play games?"

If there is one thing I have learned, it is that most of us ask the wrong questions. We need to stop spending so much energy on what's going on with the opposite sex. What about what's going on with us? What are *we* doing that influences our dating experiences and perhaps prohibits our ability to find love and get married?

What we need is to set aside enough time to improve ourselves so that there is no time to criticize the person you're dating or married to.

So many self-help books tell you just how messed up you are and give you a laundry list of insurmountable changes you'll have to make if you want to succeed. I think we are all sick of those kinds of books. The advice might be sound enough, but the practical application can be confusing and misleading simply because we are all unique individuals.

Every person is different, with a multitude of varied experiences and ways of processing them. It doesn't work to tell any one individual what to do based on what has worked for someone else. Everyone's road toward finding love is different. It is not for me or anyone else to pretend to fully understand who you are right now, where you are in the process, or what you should do next. The Holy Spirit knows you, however, and He is your guide on this journey.

Therefore, I have not written about *becoming* as some kind of strategy you can use in order to get what you want. Instead, this book is meant to serve as your own personal reality check to discover where you are incompatible with the kind of person you are hoping to attract, the kind of person who will be a suitable partner for you in Christian marriage. It will help you to look at yourself honestly to see if you're in sync with the will of God, becoming the person He has called you to be.

This book is food for thought. It is to be used as a resource for self-examination. Take the points and opinions presented and consider them prayerfully. Would *you* date you? If the honest answer is no, then trust God to help you in those particular areas.

I also want to make sure we keep things human. There is no place for perfectionistic expectations when it comes to love, marriage, or relationships. There are no perfect marriages. Every person is imperfect, and the love between two persons is imperfect. These imperfections are part of the journey that is marriage; they are not obstacles to be avoided before one can begin the journey.

When two people work on their own imperfections while embracing each other's imperfections, it is possible to have a love that lasts a lifetime. The process itself will be imperfect, but real progress can be made, depending on the efforts and decisions of the individuals involved.

You do not have to be a Christian to be successful at marital love, but Christian principles make it possible to be become the kind of person capable of something as unnatural as sustaining exclusive marital love for a lifetime. There is an impossibility about living out marriage that Jesus Christ makes possible.

To become this person requires working on yourself, and the Christian way to focus on yourself is to first focus on God. Becoming the person that God has created you to be should be your primary goal.

We must all seek to transform ourselves into persons capable of loving and being loved. To become this kind of person requires continuous conversions. Only through the love of God and the knowledge of self are we able to become lovable in the true spirit of matrimony.

A lifetime of love starts with *you*.

> The proof of love is in the works. Where love exists, it works great things. But when it ceases to act, it ceases to exist.[1]
>
> —*Pope St. Gregory the Great*

CHAPTER ONE

B e c o m e Heavenly

BEFORE WE CAN CONSIDER CERTAIN qualities to develop for the sake of our future spouse, let us first consider our end goal, which is heaven.

Ultimately, we are called to be saints by God and live with Him forever in heaven. Anything we become in this world contributes to this ultimate goal. We are destined to *become* resurrected and glorious sons and daughters of God. We are bound for heaven during this life, and we are meant to live accordingly.

As people in the world, we are busy about the things and cares of this world. It is all too easy to experience a disconnect from the spiritual life and anything beyond the here and now. As we date and eventually marry, we are distracted by many concerns regarding life with this other person. We too easily lose sight of heaven, our end goal.

One of the most significant ways we can become disconnected is when it comes to understanding the role our bodies play in getting us to heaven, and the impact of that role in dating, love, and marriage.

There is a relationship between our bodily life here on earth and our heavenly life to come. Our bodies play an important role in our getting to heaven (or hell, for that matter), and that same body will be with us throughout eternity.

Thoughts on Heaven

It might sound strange, but spending time reflecting on heaven can help singles prepare for their future marriage.

Heaven is a difficult place to comprehend. As believers, we know that if we die in a state of grace, we will go to heaven. But most of us have no idea of what we will be doing there, if we've even thought about it at all. I guess it is enough for us to do what we need to do to get there, and worry about the rest later! However, you and I need to realize that we will still be human beings in heaven. But who will we really be when we get there?

We know that we will be happy with God, and we will have new bodies. There will be no more pain, and we will not have to deal with any of our imperfections and faults any longer. But fundamentally, we will be persons in heaven, just as we are on earth. The reality that you are a *person* sets you apart from the fact of your human nature, which is collectively shared with the whole human race. And as baptized Christians, we also share the divine nature of Christ.

No two persons are the same. A person does not share his or her personhood with any other person. You are uniquely yourself. If you are a person, that means you are able to act, and you are responsible for your actions. God does not judge us collectively. He judges each person individually, based on their individual motives which can only be known to Him.

The first thing to realize about heaven is that who we will be there will be the result of our actions here on earth. To be in heaven means that our actions resulted in dying in the state of grace (God's love). But what kind of person will you be in heaven? And why should that matter to you today?

Becoming a Real Person

By nature, we are good because we are created by God. But the person we are to become is only a potential at the time of birth. Being human and becoming a person are not the same things. By birth, we are all human beings. However, becoming a whole person is a process. A baby is born with the potential of becoming a whole person. A baby is a person, but with a long way to go to be able to express full personhood. This is what makes the childhood years the development years. A seven-year-old is a little person and has developed a personality. Yet a seven-year-old is not fully a person. An eighteen-year-old is considered an adult, yet at eighteen is still not fully a person. Those in their forties can think back to when they were eighteen and realize they hardly recognize that person because they have come such a long way since then. Yet, even then, they still have further to go before they develop their full personhood.

Do you see where I am going with this? The fact is, we never stop *becoming*; therefore, we are always working toward our fullest potential as the person we are called to be until the day we die. To fully be a person means that we are in perfect harmony with God's plan for us. Falling short of that at any level and at any time means that we are less of a person. We make strides, and we have setbacks. Who we are is something that comes with the practice of living. This practice of living is what shapes us. Habits, attitudes, and personality traits are developed and influence how we act. Good habits are called virtues, and bad habits are called vices. How we act defines who we are.

Are we a virtuous person or a vicious person, or something in between? How do we know? How do others know? Our actions tell others, and ourselves, who we really are. What we do affects others, so we want to make sure that our decisions reflect who we are inside.

Everyone sins, so it cannot be just the action itself that judges us. How we recover from a sin or a failure is part of the story too.

Consistency and frequency also play a role. If you lose patience from time to time, that does not mean you are an impatient person. It takes time to discover the consistencies of a person. But it is these consistencies displayed on the outside through your actions that are the best evidence of who you are as a person.

Part of what makes you human is your fragility, your ability to fail. Your personhood is your connection to God, and all that is good. To be a bad person is to be less of a person. In fact, every bad action diminishes our personhood and causes us to become more like an animal. The dignity of every person is our goodness, our God-ness.

No person is without moments of failure. But a well-formed person will feel guilt and sorrow for wrongdoing, seek forgiveness, and make up for the wrongdoing, if possible. This person thus becomes an even better person.

It is important to realize that when you date another person, you bring all of who you are into the relationship; you are always developing into the whole person you are called to be. Working on yourself is continuous if you seek to be of value to someone else.

Expect to Be a Good Person

The person you are dating expects the best of you. He or she expects you be a good person. (Do you know anyone who seeks a serious relationship with someone they consider to be a bad person?) But how do you live up to that expectation? How do you become the good person you are meant to be?

First of all, none of us is born evil. We all reflect the image and likeness of God, the Creator. However, because sin entered the world through our first parents, evil exists. Evil is goodness gone wrong.

Every person has the potential to be good, even when they choose to do something evil. Good and evil have to do with actions of thought and of deed. When we do something evil, it affects the person we were created to be. However, as long as we are alive in this world, there is always hope in God's grace, which can overcome any evil.

Although we are innocent babies at birth, we are all sinners. The Catholic Church teaches that we cannot commit a sin until the age of reason (typically around seven years of age), because sin is related to motives and circumstances. A developing child has not yet reached the point of being able to decide with full reason. During those first seven years, the parents' teachings, the family's influence, and all experiences of that child shape the person that really starts to exist.

It is worth stressing the point here that other people shape us. Who we become does not happen in spite of other people, but rather because of them. It is important to realize that every person's interaction with a child has an effect on the person that child will become. Who they are is a result of the many people that help to shape their life.

This is why parents are exceptionally important people. They are the primary builders of their children's personalities. Everyone the parents allow to come into contact with a child contributes as well. Bad parents will establish bad qualities in their children. It is important to become a good person in order to be a good parent. We train our children to have good habits so that they will become people that are good, and do good for others, for society, for God, and for themselves. Neglecting to help a child develop good habits detracts from their personhood. Bad habits and bad character traits are the result. A person of bad character is not merely acting badly, they are failing to grow better as a person. You are created to become the best *you* possible, one who acts in ways that benefit others and God.

Socializing with other human beings is an inescapable aspect of developing into a person. Some parents, motivated by concern that their children might be badly influenced, overly shelter them. The risk of undersocialization, however, can be far greater for children than the risk that they might witness something their parent preferred they not witness. The person they become can be socially crippled, lacking the skills that are necessary to function and succeed. In the same way, a child that is allowed to spend excessive time involved with antisocial activities (e.g., computer and video games, excessive phone use, headphones in their ears, or other isolating activities) can turn out the same way. This produces antisocial and underdeveloped persons (immature adults), who may tend to remain adolescent in their behavior.

These immature, albeit adult, persons are then sent out into society. The primary societal function affected by this is the institution of marriage, and the result is bad marriages between people not capable of meeting the demands of marriage.

The Influence of Others

Just as the person you become is a result of the people you interact with during your life, the person you will be in heaven is intimately connected to other people who helped form you. This is why in heaven we will still be social beings. It won't be simply an eternity of looking at the Face of God; we will walk with those we were close to in this life, and we will meet those who influenced the persons we became.

Social interaction is necessary to form the person. Experiencing all different types of people, even those who are not attractive to us or hold very different views than ours, influences the process of becoming a good person. This is what makes good friendship such a treasured thing. A good friend enhances our personhood. We become better because of the relationship. Friendships with people who do bad or harmful things drag us down and make us worse. Therefore, our choice of who we bring into our lives is a big deal, because they play a major role in making us the person we ultimately become.

Think of how someone you know has changed because of someone they befriended. Think of how love between two people in marriage can take two good individuals and make them even better through their shared life of intimacy, trust, and experiences. This is why two people either grow happier or more miserable together. If there are problems with one person, these problems rub off on the other, often making the other less of a person as well. Soon you have two people who do not even recognize each other, and friends and family notice remarkable changes they do not like to see. But when the relationship between the two is a positive one, with genuine mutual love, there is a tremendous enhancement of each other's personalities and a happiness that is evident to those around them, particularly their children. From this love, the children have a strong foundation to become better persons themselves.

When we die, we take our progress into the next life. Everyone who has influenced us in becoming the person we have become will, we hope, be someone we see in heaven. Spouses will no longer be married, but if their love and friendship endured in the world, it will continue in heaven. If the marriage did not fare well, there should at least be no hard feelings or animosity since you will meet again in heaven (which should be mutually desired). Failing to forgive and be at peace with each other is wishing that the other will not make it to heaven, and that could result in you not making it there. One thing is for sure. Close friends will reunite and spend eternity together worshipping God. It is a beautiful image and a wonderful sign of hope for this life.

Journeying Together Toward Heaven

God chooses the people who influence our lives for good, and He chooses those whom we will influence. Because we have an influence on others, we should strive to be a positive influence by being a good person. This is the kind of person God calls us to be, and it is a call to love.

God is love; we've all heard that. But we need to keep meditating on this truth. *God is love.* There is no authentic love in this world that does not have God as the initiator and the recipient. We are privileged to participate in love, which is God. When we cooperate in this participation, powerful and beautiful things happen. The greatest human experience is sharing love. Each of us is unique. No one is like you; no one has ever been like you, nor ever will be. Each of us has value because of this uniqueness. Therefore, we can benefit in some way from every person we meet. Our actions with others not only affect who we are, they affect our relationship with God, who created us for the purpose of love. We are to love God, and love others for His sake.

It is God who brings people into your life. It is no random event when someone comes along. So be sure to pay attention to the people in your life. They are meant to enhance you as a person. How this happens is unique to your circumstances and situation. But every person you come into contact with daily was planned by God for you. Be aware that God is very involved with helping you become the person He calls you to be. Because no two people have the exact same life experiences, even one person you interact with can make a difference in the person you become. That's how subtle the path to personhood is. The one thing you can know for sure is that no matter who it is, you are called to love that person.

Remember this: You are ever-expanding as a person, because love grows immeasurably. There is nothing finite about love and nothing finite about your heart. The heart expands as love is allowed to permeate it.

The greater you love, the more fully you live as a person. The less you love, the less of a person you are. This might sound a bit depressing, because most of us assume that our attempts to show this kind of love fail more often than they succeed. However, I hope that none of you will settle on who you are right now, but will always strive to become better. Choose your friends and activities wisely, and do not allow your social life to be full of incidental things. Make the connection between interacting with people and your development as a person.

Above all, realize there is one person in this life with whom you will have the most important relationship and who will influence you the most to become the person you are called to be: the person of Jesus Christ. Becoming like Him will make the impossible possible. Our friendship with Jesus is the only reason we can successfully love everyone; we can have an intimate friendship with Christ that lasts. Very few people can find a friendship that is deep, mutual, and lasts a lifetime. Even sacred Scripture advises that it is a very rare thing indeed. But one friendship accessible to every one of us that will certainly last, and can be as deep as we are willing, is with the person of Jesus. He is always available to us, enabling us to share in His life and become like Him.

This is the path to holiness, and ultimately this is how you become the best person possible to affect the people God brings into your life.

You can fail Him, but He never fails you. Your life with Jesus always enhances and perfects you because He is always giving you more and more of Himself. He is continually changing and transforming you into the person you are called to be, primarily, another Jesus. You learn how to be good, recognizing that only God is good and that anything you do is good because of God.

When two people are very close, they are often very similar in their ways. Two people who get close to each other tend to become like each other. They start to talk the same, express themselves in the same way, and even think alike. They know each other so well, they can predict what the other will do, and they know what each other is thinking. Their love goes deep and it has an inseparable quality to it. They have truly made each other who they are because of their relationship. In the same way, the person you are should reflect Jesus in your life to others, and you should never compromise that relationship for any other person. We bring the person of Christ to others through our personhood.

You'll Still Be *You* in Heaven

So, who will you be in heaven? Well, you will be *you*. And you will be like Jesus. You will not be Jesus, but you will resemble Him because you lived as a person who loved as He loves. The decision to live His life will have been an act of your will; it will have been your decision to make. And the expression of Jesus's life through you is unique to you alone. In heaven, you will be uniquely you, still recognizable as you. You will also resemble the people with whom you shared mutual love. And the greatest resemblance you will have is to Jesus Christ, whom you loved the most and could not help but become like.

It stands to reason that we will walk in heaven with all those who affected our lives for the better. Those we were closest to in mutual love and affection on earth will be our close friends in heaven, too. It really is a beautiful thing to think about! I look forward to walking through heaven with those who have made me a better person. But above all, I look forward to walking through heaven with Jesus, whom, with God's grace, I have lived my life in this world striving to be like through love.

Some persons, sadly, have not become very good people due to experiences beyond their control. Those of us given the opportunities for goodness by God through our experiences and by grace have a responsibility to reach out to those less fortunate and be a positive influence on them. It takes only one good person to change the course of another person's life. And one day, in heaven, you will interact as persons, and as children of God.

May all the relationships we have lead us to a closer friendship with Jesus, the most important Person to influence who we are in this life and in eternity. May we all become persons who reflect the divine love that is the person of Jesus Christ, and lead others to Him through our interactions with them.

This should be the focus of your whole life as you go about the business of love and marriage. If you do not make getting to heaven the highest priority in your life, the world has the power to distract you away from God and keep you firmly in this world. Even the person you love can be a distraction if you allow them to be your end goal.

Keep heaven as your end goal, and bring that goal into all your dating experiences and eventually into your marriage. You owe it to those you date and your future spouse to live as a person bound for heaven.

CHAPTER TWO

B e c o m e Humble

HUMILITY IS TRUTH; IT IS a virtue that opens the door to every possible good experience you can provide for each other during the dating process and on into marriage. The ultimate humility for a couple is that they love each other, and that humble truth secures their bond, making it safe to live life however it comes, knowing that love will never die.

Seek a Truth-Seeker

Because humility is truth, and humility is the cornerstone of all virtue and all goodness, it is important to be a truth-seeker and find a truth-seeker in marriage.

As we go through the dating process, most of us have lots of opinions about what we are looking for in a future spouse. Most of our opinions derive from a checklist of things we want in a person we believe could make us happy. For many, at the top of their list is finding a Catholic (a serious, devout, religious person), someone who is faith-based and lives a sacramental life (goes to Mass, confession, etc.). That's good! If these things are at the top of your checklist, then you have your priorities straight.

However, it is equally important to find a truth-seeker. Sadly, there are many Catholics that are not all that interested in truth when it comes right down to it. They might do things outwardly that the Church requires, but in their day-to-day lives, they live hypocritically, or they do not bother to learn the truths of the faith and then apply them. They practice religion, but they do not desire truth.

Philosophy is the study of truth. Therefore, those who desire and seek truth are philosophers, whether they know it or not. So a truth-seeker is one who fundamentally and habitually seeks the truth, desires to discover truth, and wants to live truth.

Jesus said He was the Truth. Therefore, ultimately, a truth-seeker will find Jesus Christ, whether in the person of Jesus or in the moral code of living life that comes from Jesus. Those who seek truth desire to know what is right and wrong when it comes to living this life. They also accept that seeking truth is a process, not an event; they accept where people are on their journey toward finding truth, they are not judgmental toward others on their journey, and they understand that coming to truth is a very personal thing.

The truth is realized in a person via the Holy Spirit. And no one can know how the Holy Spirit is working in any other person. A truth-seeker is humble in knowing they have much to learn, and they should never be critical of another's struggle with truth. A truth-seeker desires to *share* what he or she learns but never to *impose* it on others.

In the dating process, finding a truth-seeker goes beyond the label of being Catholic. Claiming to be Catholic does not tell the whole story. Is this person committed to truth? That's what you need to know.

People of truth are capable of being saints in a daily world of sin. Every day we face a battle between good and evil, and we must successfully overcome a variety of temptations. This daily process fashions us into the saints we are called to become, but every day we fail at this in some way because we all sin. The good news is that every day we have an opportunity to grow, even as a result of the sins we commit. That opportunity to grow is available to everyone. If you consider yourself a truth-seeker, take every opportunity to learn the truth present in everything you face each day. A truth-seeker wakes up in the morning and asks God what He wants of him or her that day and asks for enlightenment so that truth can be followed.

To be a truth-seeker means to connect everything to the vertical relationship with God as well as the horizontal relationship with our fellow human beings. First, the vertical: In order to know the truth, the truth-seeker appeals to the divine for enlightenment of the mind, heart, and soul. Second, the horizontal: We are social beings and we have a responsibility toward our fellow human beings because of God, who created all things.

Truth-seekers ask important questions in order to learn the truth so that they can act accordingly. They are always, always connected. They make the connection between God and all that happens in their life. To be connected means to have order. This order brings a peace of soul to the truth-seeker, and they lead a holy life in every way. St. Augustine defined peace as the tranquility of order. How true this is! That means that a disordered person is not connected to God and is subsequently living life abstractly. The person who is not a truth-seeker compartmentalizes things and people in their life. They are capable of saying one thing and doing another, of acknowledging the truth but not living it, of doing all sorts of things that do not make sense as a whole, of living life out of context, of being selective about what they will and will not believe.

How does a truth-seeker differ from someone of faith who believes in God and attends Mass? The sad fact is that many individuals say they are Catholic, say they believe in God, have faith, go to Mass, or say the Rosary, and so on, but they still engage in pornography, premarital sex, masturbation, abusive behavior, resentment, objectification of others, and many other things contrary to fundamental human virtues.

How can this be? It is because of disconnected living, without a full commitment to the truth. If a person is fully committed to the truth, no matter what their sinful tendencies or weaknesses or imperfections are, they will make progress.

The most important reason to date a truth-seeker is that you will always (and I mean *always*) know that this person will, no matter what happens, have God as the higher authority he or she will ultimately answer to. You will have found someone who is humble enough to know that he or she cannot just accept their own way of thinking or acting. This person wants the truth, even if it hurts or requires them to change.

This is critical. If you marry someone who does not desire the truth, your marital challenges have the potential of perpetuating without resolve or growth due to the person of so-called faith you are now married to being stubbornly content to interpret things by their own power, conveniently insisting that they "know."

A truth-seeker can say, "I was wrong," and want to make up for it. A truth-seeker can examine himself, determine what is disordered, and take steps to restore order. A truth-seeker is quick to listen, and slow to offer opinions as absolutes. A truth-seeker respects herself and others and is not demanding. A truth-seeker does not make excuses for himself but accepts responsibility. Just because a person *says* she believes in God or goes to daily Mass, does not guarantee she is truly a person of character.

As you date, beware of someone who will not reflect on his or her own thoughts and actions, while being very quick to question yours. Do not be afraid to flat-out ask the person you are dating if they are a truth-seeker. Do they love to discover truth? Do they desire to *live* truth?

Living truth is the path to personal sanctity. I don't care how many rosaries someone says, if he or she is not a truth-seeker, that someone is not living the call to truth as Jesus proclaimed.

This is about freedom. We want to be free from error so we can live in peace. The truth will set us free. Seek truth in everything for yourself, and do not compromise having *truth-seeker* on your checklist of must-haves for a future spouse.

Codependent in a Good Way

Humility in dating means to realize the truth about what you need in a spouse as you determine whom to marry.

We live in a world of independent, self-sufficient individuals. Many single men and women don't actually *need* someone in their lives, nor do they want to give up their independence by marrying someone. Many singles have a notion that they will only marry someone who is also independent, and the two of them will decide to maintain their independence in their marriage.

The fear of being dependent on another person shows a lack of humility about love and marriage. How can you say you love someone and maintain your independence? It does not make any sense. Individuality, on the other hand, is different. We do not, and should not, lose our individuality when we love and marry. Our individuality is enhanced in marriage, but we do not stop being individuals.

Marriage enhances individuals because two people become one flesh. Marriage brings two individuals together in a bond that unifies them both under one common purpose and creates one entity. They form a company, the family, which makes them permanent partners, requiring their individual selves to be given in full for the purpose of growing the company (family). Their individuality, however, is forever changed in one very important sense; namely, they are no longer responsible only to themselves, but are now responsible to each other.

Love is about becoming codependent. The lover depends on the beloved to receive the love given. The beloved depends on the lover to give love. The individual person in a marriage partnership cannot decide they will not love or receive love at any given moment. They are always at the disposal of the other for love and for life.

The independence many singles have is a false sense of freedom. A woman might fear giving up her independence because she thinks marriage will somehow prevent her ability to do whatever she wants. Well, that's true enough. However, doing whatever we want is not freedom. Loving God is true freedom, and to love God is to live as God wills, which is by love itself. Love is a gift of self. Therefore, we are never truly free unless we are giving ourselves in love to others.

This does not necessarily mean marital love. Any opportunity we have to love one another in charity or service is an exercise in freedom. But a single person has the sense of personal independence because they can step in and out of love for others as they see fit. They can spend plenty of time and money on themselves. They can be selfish and get away with it.

In marriage, you cannot get away with selfishness. There are no selfish people in heaven, so marriage is specifically designed by God to take your independence and transform it into a life of selfless giving.

Why marry at all, though, if you are happily selfish in your independent life? One answer is that, whether you know it or not, you need to be needed. You need a codependent. There is nothing wrong with needing someone. This does not mean that you should be a needy, clingy person—that's something different. To need someone is to have someone you can depend on in the life you set out to build together. A good partnership is successful specifically because the partners know they depend on each other, and that sense of responsibility inspires each person to do his or her part.

Singles should not be dating if they are not willing to eventually trade in their independence for a life of dependency. It is not fair to the other person, and it shows a lack of understanding of what love really is.

To be humble in dating is to acknowledge that you need a good partner with whom you can establish a family and share a lifetime. The truth is that you want to love and be loved, and that love makes you and your partner dependent on each other. You can help each other maintain and grow in your individuality, and you can encourage each other in interests you have independent of one another. But you absolutely must be able to depend on each other in everything.

Humility in dating accepts that marriage is about one life lived by two people who are bonded by love for a lifetime. Do not fear losing your independence. Your ability to love and be loved depends on leaving your independence at the altar on your wedding day and embracing the dependency you establish as you say your vows.

Our Lord said that the truth will set you free (see John 8:32). As a truth-seeker, you realize that to depend on another person in marriage is true freedom because you have a lifetime commitment to give yourself in love to each other. To love yourself is enslavement. To love another is freedom.

Beware the Inner Pharisee

Does the person you are dating strike you as someone with an overly high moral, educational, or even cultural standard? Do you feel like your every action is being observed? Is this person overly critical of you? Is he quick to find fault with you but not with himself? Does she make you feel like your level of religious practice or approach to life is not on par with hers? Do you get the impression your past sins are interpreted as who you are now?

If you answered yes to any of these, then you might be dating a Pharisee.

The Pharisees of Jesus's time were the authorities of the Jewish community who imposed strictness on living out the letter of the law down to the smallest detail. They did not practice what they preached. It was a hypocrisy that Jesus had no tolerance for.

In fact, Jesus presented a chilling parable depicting a Pharisee and a tax collector in the Temple praying (see Luke 18:9–14). The Pharisee boldly says, "God, I thank you that I am not like other people—robbers, evildoers, adulterers—or even like this tax collector. I fast twice a week and give a tenth of all I get." The simple tax collector stayed at a distance and would not even look up to heaven, but beat his breast and said, "God, have mercy on me, a sinner." Jesus says that the tax collector, who was humble, went home justified, while the Pharisee, who was self-righteous, did not.

Was this a bit too harsh of Jesus? Not at all. Jesus is not impressed with those who are confident in their own favor with God while they look down on others and are quick to judge. How bold for the

Pharisee to point to the tax collector in the Temple, telling God he was glad he was not like him, assuming the tax collector was full of hypocrisy when it was really the Pharisee who was the hypocrite.

But it should make us all tremble, because there is a little bit of the Pharisee in all of us that has to constantly be recognized and worked on. We hold others up to very high standards and even recoil when someone falls short of those expectations (maybe even cut someone off for their failure). Yet, we have an incredible capacity for justifying our own actions and even blinding ourselves to the hypocritical approach to the life we lead.

This does not bode well for building successful relationships with others. How can another person live up to all of our expectations? And if they cannot, does that mean that they are unworthy of our friendship or our love? There is no doubt that there are actions, behaviors, and sins, that are deal-breakers for a relationship. But there are many great relationships made up of two good, yet imperfect, people.

A person might have a past or a particular problem or certain weaknesses that can infiltrate the relationship at times and cause the couple to question the sustainability of their relationship. This is where the Pharisee in us can creep in and cause the most problems. When trouble arises, no matter how grave it is, we focus on what the other has done. We hold that person up against the strictest of rules and judge them accordingly. In our hurt, we ask, "How could you?"

At this point it is critical to begin asking yourself some honest questions. "Am I capable of doing such a thing?" "Did I do something to contribute to this?" Without an introspective component to a troubled time in a relationship, the Pharisee in us will take over, imposing its stringent (and often cruel) position on the offending party.

At the same time, the offending party might believe that *they* are the offended party, causing defensiveness. The result is that two Pharisees emerge, taking over the situation in such a way that resolution is impossible. Both Pharisees need to be extinguished before there can be a resolution. Both parties have to take an honest look at how they might have contributed to the situation. Each party will have to get to the point of considering how to be compassionate toward the other. This is what the Lord meant when he taught that we must get the beam out of our own eye before trying to remove the splinter from someone else's.

That analogy is very significant. It implies that we are always the worst of the parties involved. This suggests two things:

1. Neither person in a relationship should be so focused or anxious about how wrong the other person is.
2. It is not your job to fix the other person.

The Pharisee in us is a tyrant that desires to control another person while making excuses for ourselves. This Pharisee wants the other person to live up to our every expectation without that person imposing any kind of expectations on us. The more we express the Pharisee in us, the more we are blinded by our own harmful thoughts and actions.

In my work, I think I've heard about every kind of relationship problem there is. In almost all cases, the problem can be traced to the fact that one person in the relationship is a Pharisee. So many relationship problems are really individual problems.

For example, a Pharisee is dating someone who has lived a lie. The Pharisee knows that deception is wrong and presses that person to explain their past and justify it. The Pharisee goes as far as to feel so offended by this perfectly wonderful, repentant person's past that he or she ends the relationship. Perhaps the Pharisee believes that once a deceiver, always a deceiver. Yet, the Pharisee has a track record of deception as well that has been justified as not being the same thing, or maybe they deny it all together, thus living a life of self-deceit.

The opposite of how a Pharisee operates is humility. In humility, there is self-recognition rather than self-deception. There is a readiness to forgive because the humble person knows he or she has been forgiven. There is a commitment to forget another person's past and embrace who they are now. The humble person considers others better than himself because he knows he has sinned more than anyone. And with humility there is always a desire to be merciful first, especially if someone feels sorrow over what has happened, because mercy is at the heart of love, which is the heart of Christ.

Dating couples need to work at making each other feel relaxed so that authentic love has a chance to develop and blossom. They should be quick to see the best in each other, and assume any fault within themselves, rather than thinking the worst about the other person and playing the victim.

God blesses and exalts the humble. Work on diminishing and exposing the Pharisee in yourself, and you will learn to love with the eyes and heart of Christ.

CHAPTER THREE

B e c o m e **Prayerful**

MANY SINGLES ARE INTERESTED IN finding love and getting married, and many of them are serious about their religious beliefs and sharing that faith with someone in marriage. They naturally turn to prayer, asking God to send them that special, perfect person who will be their spouse.

However, for many of us, prayers are merely petitions for wants that are not preceded by a close friendship with God. When this is the case, we are susceptible to seeing prayer as a way to gauge God based on direct answers to our petitions. Did I get what I prayed for or not? If not, God must not hear my prayer, or I have done something to cause God not to grant me what I want.

An authentic prayer life, by contrast, sees God as the companion of our souls and our every moment, regardless of what happens. This friendship with God is as important as breathing, and it does not depend on answered petitions to maintain its steady, peaceful coexistence with this loving friend of our soul.

Examine Your Motives

Being serious about your faith does not assure you of having a close friendship with God. Religious practices and devotions are tools that assist in the development of authentic prayer. Too often, we misinterpret these practices as a sign of spiritual growth, when in fact it is very possible to be going backward and becoming less spiritual even while attending daily Mass or saying the rosary every day.

Our foundation should be a desire to practice our faith seriously based on prayer that is purely about loving God. By this I do not mean we should become some holy card picture of a saint in ecstasy with a halo. Each of us is capable of being aware of God at every moment. This kind of prayer life fashions a practical holiness that makes for better relationships with other human beings, particular the unique relationship of two spouses in marriage.

Those of us who love God know very well that we do not love Him as much as we should, nor do we include Him in our everyday life as we should. Jesus told us to pray without ceasing for an important reason: he knows our weakness. Praying constantly seems unfathomable, impossible to do, and probably crazy to most of us.

But this is truly how we need to approach our lives—not just seriously, but prayerfully. When you have dated others, how often have you witnessed (either in yourself or in the other person) inconsistency with what is professed as belief and what is demonstrated by words and behavior?

Christians who are dating often become confused and get damaged or discouraged because the expectation of taking Christian life seriously is tainted when they experience rudeness, a lack of charity, insensitivity, and all manner of things contrary to love as Jesus taught it. The seriousness of dating in order to find a marriage partner is unsuccessful because the individuals involved are not serious about being Jesus to each other.

Being like Jesus and bringing Him to others is serious business, and it must be undertaken seriously and prayerfully. Jesus wanted us to know that if we are going to be like Him and share His very life consistently, we must pray without ceasing.

The more prayer permeates our life, the more Christlike we are. If we are not prayerful, we are left to ourselves, which means sin is not far behind.

Dating is frustrating for many because it does not seem to be a very Christian experience. You see individuals who *are* Christian just kind of putting that aside while they take care of things they feel are more important—like their selfish desires and personal pleasures. After all, God wants us to be happy, right? So we should date with a mind-set to find someone who makes us happy, right?

Well, perhaps. But not at the expense of the true purpose of dating, which is entering into the vocation of marriage, and not at the expense of someone's dignity. Every person we date deserves too be treated with Christian love.

Learn to Pray in the Moment

We should be praying at every step along the dating path, including during each date and between dates. We should ask the Lord, the Holy Spirit, Our Lady, our Guardian Angel, or anyone in heaven or purgatory, for help as to what say next, for knowing the proper thing to do, for protection from a temptation, or for the ability to smile when we might be inclined to say something rude.

How many people do this kind of praying while on their dates? My guess is not many. They just wing it and hope for the best.

This is very risky, primarily because we are prone to sin and to messing things up, but also because this approach can disconnect us from our moral compass. I am sure many people feel they are good Catholics and pray for God's assistance, and they think that means they have enough in place to be okay on their own as they interact with others.

Of course, some are able to do this better than others because they have developed virtue and the resulting good social habits. But even those persons need to be attentive to what they say and do, and they should strive to remain connected to the divine as they interact with people.

Most of us, though, have too many bad habits in the way we speak and act that require us to be careful and to invoke divine assistance in the moment, not just at the beginning or end of the day. For those who are dating, this is imperative. Our selfishness is always at work to dominate our interpersonal relationships, so the connection to God and His angels and saints will go a long way in steering us appropriately through these relationships, especially when making first impressions.

Here are some examples of what might be petitioned in the moment on a date:

- "Help me stop focusing on the physical, and pay attention to the whole person."
- "Help me to overcome my initial feeling to pull back, and give this fellow Christian my full attention."
- "Help me to recover from not liking what was just said and restore your peace in me."
- "Help me refrain from staring lustfully at this woman, or looking at other women while I'm with this one."
- "Help me to resist correcting what he said or from dominating the conversation."
- "Help me to stop talking about myself and show more interest in this person."

• "Help me not judge the way this person speaks (or eats, or exhibits certain mannerisms) too harshly."

Praying at all times is the way to keep yourself on the straight and narrow. You can still be yourself, but praying through your day can enhance your better self and tame your lesser self. Do not consider this impossible or too hard. The grace is there. It can be done. It just takes practice. Keep your prayers short and simple. Simply ask for help when you recognize you need it. And help *will* come. It is a worthwhile habit to develop, one that will make all the difference in having success in your dating life.

Persevere in Prayer

Do you have perseverance? Do you really (and I mean really) believe that your prayers will cause God to act on your behalf?

I know for a fact that many single people are praying to God for a good spouse. (And those who are not should be.) God must be involved in the process, since He is the author of authentic love. Those who long to be married and pray for it are earnestly asking God to bring them the one who they are to marry.

Yet, for some these prayers seem to go unanswered. Despite a strong desire to be married, they still find themselves unmarried. They ask questions like, "What am I doing wrong?" "Why does it happen for others but not for me?" and, "Why won't God answer my prayer?"

These are natural questions. We might try to answer someone who is struggling by saying, "trust in God." This is good advice, but typically not very comforting to hear. The person wants to get married, and they want to know why God is not making it happen.

I empathize with those who want to be married. And I find it is very difficult to find anything comforting to say. But there is one thing that one must be very careful of, and that is frustration. Frustration is a sign of fallen trust. We do not want to admit this, but it is true. When we get frustrated, we start to commit to the direction of anger and resentment that slowly develops, often unnoticed. This is the direction that says, "It is not going *my* way." We want to control our own destiny. We feel we have a right to have things go as planned. Frustration, anger, and resentment take away our peace and strip us of our focus on God. When we lose our joy in serving Him, we are no longer choosing to be childlike and allowing God to be our Father.

When frustrations of any kind emerge, in humility you must declare that you do not trust in God as you should. You should speak to God in that very moment saying, "Lord, help me." Ask for peace and acceptance. When we do not maintain childlike trust, confidence, and dependence on God as Father, our choice means He cannot be the Father He desires to be.

That is the precise point of prayer. Prayer displays a childlike humility, and God responds to that. The greater the faith behind the prayer, the more efficacious God's response can be. Prayer offered that does not have much expectation behind it does not motivate God to answer the prayer. Why should He? If you do not really believe, then answering the prayer as you want is not in your best interests. Jesus taught us that our faith is the critical ingredient. Trust in God is an act of faith.

The Key to Answered Prayer

There is one more thing that is necessary for answered prayer, and that is living a clean life. If we are living life in a way that is not in accordance with God's will, then we cannot expect to have our prayers answered. Once you are focused on your life in Christ, begin to pray like you already know it will happen. It is just a matter of *when*. It is justice for a good person living a clean life and staying close to God to have their prayers answered.

St. Thérèse of Lisieux taught us how to remain childlike, expecting all things from God. St. Monica taught us perseverance. It took her thirty years of prayer before her son, St. Augustine, was converted to the Catholic faith. I am sure that after twenty years, she could have legitimately said, "Lord, I think that is a sufficient amount of time, don't you?"

So remember this key to prayer as you pray for a good spouse, or anything else in your life. Live your life in accordance with God's will, actually ask for what you want, persevere, and have a childlike faith. Live your life as one who is thankful to God and confident He is going to grant your request.

Jesus is clear that under these conditions, God the Father cannot and will not deny His own children. Don't ever get discouraged in prayer. Maintain faith, because you never know what is in God's plan. God might require a certain amount of time for the same prayer before He finally acts, but this is His way of increasing our faith.

Be steadfast and do not lose heart. Keep praying to God for your future spouse with consistency. God will not be outdone in generosity. Keep showing Him your great trust and faith until He is convinced you are ready to receive what you ask for.

Hypocrisy in Prayer

Jesus states, "Not everyone who says to me, 'Lord, Lord' shall enter the kingdom of heaven, but he who does the will of my Father who is in heaven" (Matthew 7:21). He goes on to say that there will be those who say they prophesied or drove out demons or did mighty deeds in His name. But Jesus is not impressed. "Did you do the will of my Father?"

This is the question we will all be asked. We will not be able to stand there and say, "But I went to Mass every day," or, "I gave 10 percent of my money to the Church," or ,"I spent lots of my free time volunteering for good causes," if at the same time we lived a consistent life of sin that we knew was not in accordance with God's will.

Perhaps you willingly engage in pornography, have premarital sex, steal from your company, lie to people, cheat on your taxes, overcharge someone in the name of business, disobey the speed limit, break legitimate civil laws, gossip about others habitually, or are mean-spirited to such a degree that you are inclined to think and talk negatively of others.

There are people who use prayer as their excuse for doing some pretty lousy things to other people that they, of course, have decided are good things. And there are those who use their religion to excuse their questionable practices, or they question your actions and accuse you of not being Christian. For example, a Catholic business owner cheats you or does shoddy work, and then seems to assume that because they were Catholic you should not question their work.

We all must guard against this kind of hypocrisy and disconnection. It is all too easy to compartmentalize our values, beliefs, and principles to suit our purposes while not adhering to an absolute commitment to the objective truth and the decision to live it out once realized.

The Dualistic Man

The Dualistic Man is a human being (man or woman) who attempts to live in two worlds at the same time. In one world the Dualistic Man plays God and does whatever it is he desires. In the other world, he has to do what is expected of him, and he does his best to conceal the secret world he has created.

Many men and women who live this kind of dualism have done it for so long they do not even realize they are doing it anymore. It is just who they are. They are shocked and surprised when someone discovers something about their secret world. It is not the *real* world, so why would anyone take anything they do in that world seriously, or judge them by it?

Many of us have come across this phenomenon in everyday life, especially in dating experiences. You hear a person speak so wonderfully about very important things like living the Catholic faith or other important topics of life, and he or she seems so normal, so grounded. Then you discover this person has been doing something contrary to what they talked about, and it leaves you confused, or even hurt.

This is the Dualistic Man in action. They create a world without consequences. It is a world they can enter into at will in order to be someone that they know they cannot be in the real world.

What happens, sadly, is that they get to the point where they cannot distinguish between the secret and the real world and thus lose themselves.

You might be surprised to hear that every one of us has some level of the Dualistic Man in them. This is simply because we all sin. None of us would sin if we knew we could not get away with it. We sin precisely because we feel justified in doing something. It is present in our minds in that secret world where actions have no consequences.

Happily, for many of us, we are quickly jolted out of this secret world because of our well-informed consciences that convict us of the sin, produce sufficient sorrow and guilt, and prompt us to make things right again. That is called grace. And the more we live the life of grace, the less frequent our visits to the secret world become.

Many others, unfortunately, have spent too much time in this secret world and have developed the habit of living a dualistic life. They need a great deal of help to end this unhealthy existence, especially if they ever hope to enter into the vocation of marriage and, even more importantly, enter into the kingdom of heaven.

Pray Simply, Live Simply

The remedy is a simple, prayerful approach to life. Simplicity in attitude, in the way we live, in the way we deal with others, in the way we approach God. Simplicity and focus bring clarity to our minds and peace to our lives. Do the will of the Father, and you will be happy. And guess what? You will also be a person of prayer. This shows your love for God, and He in turn blesses you abundantly. Jesus made Himself available to us completely so that we could do the will of His Father in heaven.

We all owe it to God and to ourselves, and also to the people we date and the one person we hope to love and marry one day, to pray every day to fulfill God's will so that we will grow in grace and holiness and receive such blessings as the gift of love and marriage.

Our Lord said to live every day as if it were our last. Can you say at the end of this day that you have done everything in accordance with God's will? If not, make your peace with Him and beg Him for the strength to amend your life in every way necessary so that your life will be simplified, focused, and prayerful.

CHAPTER FOUR

B e c o m e **Pure**

IMPURITY IS NOT JUST A result of what the body does. In fact, the body could do nothing pure without the purity of the mind and heart to direct it. To become pure starts with our interior self where we think and decide. Our motives, intentions, and imagination contribute to our thinking and decision-making process.

Motive, Intent, and Imagination

Our five senses are the vehicles used to deliver information. The mind and heart process the information and send out instructions to the body based on how this information is processed. To become pure means using the five senses with care and prudence and developing a spiritual life that influences how the information is processed.

Jesus taught, "Blessed are the pure in heart, for they shall see God" (Matthew 5:8). *See God* think about that! I don't think Jesus was pulling a fast one on us. I don't think He wanted us to second-guess His plain words. He said those who are pure will "see God." Who wouldn't want to see God while on this earth? Jesus made it very simple. The more pure you become, the more you will be able to see God.

This is a promise of transparency. Purity provides clear vision. As you become pure, the eyes of your soul become much clearer about the realities of God, which causes a transformation in how you live your life. As you see God in everything, your life changes accordingly.

What a beautiful reality! The problem is that our five senses contain tremendous liabilities that can disrupt this vision, sometimes to the point of total blindness. Our motives, intentions, and imagination can become so tainted and disordered that the mind cannot think properly, and the heart cannot love affectively. If you just consider what movies, music, advertising, and pornography alone have done to destroy purity, you can begin to understand why so many have trouble seeing God in their lives or in themselves.

We have to become single-minded and radically cleanse ourselves from everything that threatens our purity or causes us to have bad motives, from everything that might provide unholy and evil content for our imagination.

Dating is severely affected by impurity. You just never know who you are dating, and it is not easy to discover if a person is committed to impurity. It is not healthy to date with suspicion or skepticism, however. It is good to trust and hope, and just be yourself. But be observant. The signs will be there. It is okay to ask questions, too, as long as you are not coming across like you are on a witch hunt. Impurity is widespread and has many levels, but we are people of faith and we believe in the grace of God. Anyone can turn around. Anyone can become pure and start to see God.

But as you can see, impurity is primarily interior. And one of the worst offenses against purity is impure motives. So don't get caught up in equating purity with something only related to sex. Even if people have been taught that premarital sex is wrong, a sin and offense against God, there can still be a major ignorance that keeps them from retaining their virginity. That ignorance has to do with the will and one's ability to control oneself in the face of temptation, coupled by a lack of connection between one's humanity and the Divine. Premarital sex is a huge temptation. No one can survive this temptation without having developed the virtue of self-control.

Without a well-developed will, weakness can take over the undisciplined person, causing them to fall. The person prone to give in to premarital sex has disconnected themselves from the Divine. They have a compartment for God with select ways they love Him, and a separate compartment that stores their own desires. This means they are living a dual life. Instead of destroying the compartmentalizing approach to God, they foster the dualism in order to justify their poor choices. They have to! How else can a Christian who claims to love God get away with such actions?

I have met many well-meaning Catholics who suffer from dualism and an undisciplined will, and most of them do not even realize it. We all have a responsibility to seek truth and take advantage of the sacraments that help us rise above life's setbacks. God is always inviting us to know Him better, be honest with ourselves, and make the decision to choose Him above all else.

Jesus Christ is really present in the Eucharist, and His image on a crucifix is a visual reminder of the ultimate witness of self-control and the connection between the human and the Divine. Keep the Eucharistic Lord in your heart and at the center of your life. That is ultimately how you will become pure, remain chaste, and not waiver from your position.

The Body and Preserving Chastity

With a chapter on purity, you might expect me to mention specific matters related to the topics of premarital sex and chastity. There is no doubt that I could, but I prefer not to reinvent the wheel. There are vast amounts of information available that is easily accessible. I certainly encourage you to take the time to learn as much as possible that is in line with Christian principles and Church teachings about the subjects on sex and chastity.

But I can't let it go completely, so I will share a few things that might be helpful to singles, although these principles should be upheld for a lifetime, whether a person is single or in a marriage.

To become pure, you must protect your body. It's as simple as that. If you are careless about this, you will not be able to protect yourself against what your body does in rebellion. Scripture, the Church, and spiritual writers historically attest to the fact that the flesh is weak, and so an unruly body will take over and rule us. The spirit must rule the flesh. The body is beautiful, but it is weak, and it wants to be in control.

How do we take this very serious reality and incorporate it into the much more lighthearted and attractive life of the body we call dating? Our bodies must interact with other bodies when we date. There is no way around that. By interact, I simply mean that as human persons, we all have bodies and we go on dates with persons who also have bodies. Our bodies are the only vehicles we have to help us get to know another person. It helps to be aware ahead of time that the body of the person we are dating wants to control that person, just as our body wants to control us. Not exactly dinner conversation, but at least an unspoken mutual understanding.

Dating is a process, with expectations within this process. The first expectation is that both people are open to finding their future spouse. They are spending time with each other specifically because they want to determine if the other might be the person for their future marriage. The second expectation is that both people are serious about staying close to God and having a chaste dating experience. Romance, friendship, and intimacy can be expressed chastely before marriage without immoral actions.

Romance and friendship build intimacy. They also build sexual desire. This is where our bodies start looking for a chance to seize control. Once sexual desire is aroused, new things have to be addressed, including preserving chastity and considering marriage. Romance during the dating process is focused on making the other feel special and uniquely loved.

Building a friendship is much more important than romance. To marry someone you can count on, feel secure with, and trust, someone you cannot imagine spending your life without, is a precious gift. Friends hurt each other, but they are always there for you. You can count on them. Friends do not come and go based on moods or feelings. They can be trusted to be your friend, even when you might not be a good friend yourself. This trust is a cornerstone to any future marriage. It is almost more important to hear the one you love say, "I trust you," than, "I love you." The words "I love you," are said freely, even recklessly, today. But to hear the words, "I trust you," would have quite an impact.

How we conduct ourselves is a reflection of our interior life. Therefore, the way we speak, the way we dress, and the way we behave all bear witness to what is in our minds, hearts, and spiritual lives. By committing ourselves to becoming pure, we take seriously the role of the body in forming our interior life.

Purity in body is fundamental to preserving chastity and respecting the person you love. While dating, purity in body is essential to growing as a couple as well as an individual. Sins of bodily impurity are arguably the most common and most understandable sins. The body does what the mind does not want it to do. Human weakness is exceptionally prevalent when it comes to temptations that threaten bodily purity.

Modern society has absolutely no tolerance for the concept of purity. In fact, it is almost as if the concept of being bodily pure makes you unwelcome and puts you outside the normal life of the community. Being an outsider is always a lonely feeling. No one wants to be excluded. Yet, when it comes to purity, we must be committed to being countercultural, even if we have to stand alone as the only person defending purity. This is truly a martyrdom of sorts.

To become pure is to know who you are and preserve that dignity despite the accepted impurity of the culture you live in or the people in your life.

Modesty

One must consider how modesty plays a role in presenting the real you externally. The real you is both body and spirit. They cannot be separated. Your body outwardly represents who you are. No one can legitimately say that it does not matter what you wear, what you say, or how you conduct yourself, that it is only what's inside that matters.

No, what's outside matters too. In fact, the outside tells the story of what is inside. Or at least, it tells a story, if not *the* story. What is the story you want to tell about yourself publicly? There is an old saying that goes, "You might be the only Bible someone ever reads." We could rephrase that by saying, "You might be the only Jesus Christ someone ever encounters."

What people observe about you *does* have an effect. And people should care about how people perceive them. We cannot control what people say or think about us, and we can't worry about it, but we should care that what is being observed about us is an accurate representation of who we are. If they get it wrong, that's not your fault. Just make sure *you* get it right.

That brings up the topic of modesty. Modesty is not so much about clothes as it is about intent. It is not so much what is worn, but how it is worn, as well as the attitude that goes along with the presentation.

Don't get me wrong. Certain clothing is objectively immodest. But for a woman to be immodest, she must be at risk of looking provocative. So a woman who is not trying to be immodest, or who believes that, in fact, she is not being immodest, can still be objectively immodest by the fact that certain clothing she is wearing presents her in a way that compels men to notice her.

To lust after a woman is to desire her in a sexual, physical, and inappropriate way. A man's desire to have sex with a woman he is simply looking at is, by definition, lust. It is a man's responsibility to practice self-control and self-mastery in order to not be inclined to lust after a woman. Plenty of modestly dressed women are beautiful and desirable looking. A woman cannot be made to take full blame for a man desiring her.

Christian men are legitimately frustrated that they are exposed to women who dress provocatively. Certain clothes on certain body types are going to be eye-catching. Women know this, and quite frankly, they have enough vanity at times to enjoy it. It is natural for a woman to want to be noticed and considered beautiful. I highly doubt, however, that you can find a Christian woman who would say she is happy if a man lusts after her.

The dilemma today is that women live in a culture where they can get away with dressing in a variety of ways without knowing the fine line between modesty and immodesty, and men who have the problem of loving this and hating it at the same time. How can a man not love seeing a woman dressed seductively? Yet at the same time, a man might feel bad for being so seemingly shallow.

The truth is that clothes are not the only contributor. A woman's hair and makeup contribute to her overall outward appearance too. But the worst of it is the attitude behind it all.

A woman may wear a sleeveless dress that also exposes her legs and knees. How she does her hair and makeup, and how she conducts herself in that dress can make the difference between modesty and immodesty. Even a woman in a pair of jeans and a long-sleeved sweater can look provocative if she conducts herself in a manner that is meant to turn men's heads.

The movie *We Bought a Zoo* stars actress Scarlett Johansson. Ms. Johansson is known as a woman of exceptional beauty and sex appeal. Most publicity photos and magazine shoots present her quite immodestly, obviously intending to highlight her physical attributes. In this movie, however, she was nothing close to that. She was not unattractive, but she did not have any of the seductive presentation of her public persona. She was pretty but average looking, and definitely not wowing. Her character in *He's Just Not That into You* lives up the public persona we are more familiar with.

Ms. Johansson's character in *We Bought a Zoo* proves that a beautiful, even sexy, woman can attractively present and conduct herself in a way that will not easily and obviously lure the eyes of men, nor stir their minds to impure or lustful thoughts. In fact, a Christian woman should not want to be a source of temptation and should strive to consciously avoid this as far as she is able. She should be aware of the clothes she wears, and how her hairstyle and makeup combine with her clothes to create an effect. She should definitely not intend to get noticed via the way she walks, talks, or looks at men.

All of these things contribute to immodesty. It's not just about how much flesh is showing. How a woman conducts herself publicly also can contribute to a lack of modesty.

Does it sound like I am saying that Christian women should hide their beauty and dress frumpy and wear no makeup? On the contrary! A pretty woman can be a pretty woman without flaunting herself. Women must be honest with themselves about their vanity. Many women have a strong temptation to vanity that leads to immodesty. True humility allows a beautiful woman to be honest about her outward appeal and act accordingly in the name of the Lord.

Instead, too many women act in the name of themselves and tell others to just deal with it. This is not a Christian attitude. Women must consider the effect they have on men and be circumspect about their outward presentation and conduct.

Men should also be modest in the way they present themselves. One major thing men do immodestly is lead women to believe they are interested in them when they are not.

But for most men, particularly Christian men, the struggle is in processing the actions of women. Modesty would encourage a man to guard his eyes or speak up when necessary to share his preference not to be exposed to anything immodest. Though immodesty in women is an inevitable part of daily life for men, they have to strive not to underreact or overreact improperly. Modesty calls them to self-control.

A good Christian man does not want a woman he lusts after. He might deceive himself in thinking he wants a *hot* woman. Those who truly care only for a woman's looks are not good Christian marriage material. No, what a good Christian man wants is a modest woman who conducts herself in a manner befitting her faith, respectful of the one man who is the only man she wants to have admire her and have her in any sensual way. She does not seek to purposely parade herself to the general male populace. She makes sure her man knows that she cares only that he desires her, not anyone else.

A woman can be modest and still look classy and elegant, not trampy and seductive. She can be beautiful without every man wanting her. She can dress in a way that complements her body without showing it off. She can behave in ways that show she is self-confident in her looks, without assuming her looks are to be noticed and admired by all.

Modesty starts with the love of God and being thankful for how God made you. It grows in an attitude of charity about how to present and conduct yourself. Modesty in dating and courtship allow a woman to use her looks and charm to win the heart of one man and exercise extreme care to make him comfortable and secure that her looks are only for him.

The Gatekeeper of Chastity

I would like to mention something related to premarital sex that is not often considered, and I offer it as food for thought. I personally believe there is a rock-solid gatekeeper of chastity that, if understood with respect and practiced with virtuous self-control and discipline, is the key to safeguarding bodily purity as it relates to sexual activity. That something is the act of kissing.

When it comes to kissing or other forms of physical touch before marriage, opinions about when to kiss and what are appropriate kinds of kissing during dating vary greatly. There are also different ideas of how kissing is connected to maintaining virginity.

Purity demands a careful consideration of how kissing can affect purity, especially how it can compromise it. It might seem strange to make such a fuss about kissing when there are much more dangerous things to worry about concerning purity. But as you will see, kissing holds a significant key to whether or not the other dangerous things occur.

Kissing is not just something we do. It is an expression of our interior. Obviously, kissing is natural and good. But there are different types of kissing, and it is important to realize that there are some forms of kissing that belong only in marriage, not during courtship. The most common three types of kissing are 1) the peck on the cheek, 2) the pressing of lips, and 3) the more passionate expression of kissing known as French kissing, where the tongue is involved.

I think we can immediately eliminate the peck on the cheek option as being anything negative. Kissing someone on the cheek displays a sign of affection, but hardly qualifies as something immoral or that would break down the defenses of purity that maintain one's virginity. Friends and family express their love for each other this way (including men with other men in many cultures).

Kissing by pressing each other's lips enters the realm of the sacred, in my view. I am sure many will think I am crazy, or perhaps old-fashioned, but the more I understand about personhood, marriage, purity, and love, the more I think we are too flippant about the act of kissing on the lips. This is a very intimate event, no matter how innocent. It should at least hold some kind of basic value to the individuals involved. It's not simply a kiss for fun, and it certainly is not an empty gesture. Just ask any girl what they think of a kiss, and most will tell you it has more meaning than if you just shook hands. It is an unspoken language. It is communication. And what is communicated depends on how it is interpreted, so it's worth having enough respect for lip kissing to not be loose and careless about it.

So, is it wrong to give a little kiss to someone you are dating? In one respect, not at all. If we're still talking about a kiss on the lips, I would agree that it's harmless enough. The quick kiss two young people might do because they are shy, curious, and young has an innocent charm to it. Where it starts to get dangerous is the kiss on the lips for a longer duration of time. There is nothing wrong with this. I don't believe closed-mouth kisses are typically capable of exciting passions that lead to other physical activity, including those that would break down the defenses of purity that maintain one's virginity. Unless, of course, the arms get involved. If you hug and press each other close for an extended period of time while kissing, the risk of exciting passions increases, starting with the temptation to open the mouth and move on to the next kind of kiss.

But let us stay with closed-mouth kissing for a moment. Let us agree that it is not wrong, per se, nor immoral. However, there is symbolism to this action that needs to be considered. The prolonged kiss on the lips is a gesture that represents something more (or at least it should). It represents a willing offering of the heart. Particularly for a woman, a kiss represents the invitation to pursue the relationship further.

Men should greatly respect this aspect of a woman, and a good man is going to feel the same way. The alternative is the risk of heartbreak on either side, men as well as women. If there was kissing involved in a relationship that ends, no matter how brief, there is more given away than just the lips. That kiss contains affection that is rooted in the heart.

Every young girl dreams of her first kiss. Boys typically do not. They simply want to kiss a girl. Girls want to fall in love. The kiss is a symbol of that possibility. Boys just want to kiss for the pleasure of it.

Girls want it to be so much more than that. And they have the power to inspire boys to feel that way too. In that respect, a woman can lead a man in chastity. But a man who has this sensibility and lives it in his dating life inspires the heart of a woman.

Saving your kiss for your future spouse may be difficult (if not impossible) for the modern world to practice, but it is wise to try. Kissing is definitely a precursor. Preserving your kiss also helps preserve your virginity for your future spouse. It means those who just want sex from you will flee pretty quickly. And that's good, because that means you learned their moral quality, which is not much if they are not willing to wait. *You* are worth the wait.

The physical action of kissing is the first line of defense, and to express a physical kiss is to challenge the guards. Once past this guard, other physical allowances will then be challenged and succumbed to.

Let this external expression happen, and the interior will is weakened. The more you do it, the weaker your will becomes. It is folly to assume that purity can be maintained with passionate kissing. Perhaps there are rare people who have such strong self-control that they can kiss deeply and stop there. But most of us cannot. There really is no place for this kind of kissing among two practicing, single Christians. It is too dangerous, and our call to chastity requires that we guard against stirring the passions.

I suggest focusing on the principle of kissing. More single persons should be aware of this and be able to make the connection between the kiss and the heart. This is especially necessary for men when it comes to a woman's heart. We need more virgins coming to the altar of the Lord on wedding days. I am convinced that kissing has a lot to do with why there are not more people who have saved themselves for their wedding day.

I realize those who are dating today are faced with the expectation to have sex, even among Catholics, and I am aware that my opinion on kissing seems unrealistic. We live in a sex-obsessed world. Sadly, a kiss is not considered sacred, just as virginity is not. Why not bring back the gesture of a man kissing a woman's hand? It is charming, it is respectful, it is gentlemanly, and it is very attractive. It also preserves purity while still expressing affection through a kiss.

I recognize that people kiss people they do not end up marrying. I do not want to imply that I think you are wrong, or bad, or immoral if you engage in kissing someone you do not marry. It is not a matter of what is morally wrong or right. I just want to challenge you to give this some thought and consider something countercultural that might actually enhance dating and marriage. It is a matter of strengthening your will, because a weak will easily makes excuses for actions. Consider what is important, consider your motives, and consider the motives behind an action long before you decide to do something. This just might help protect your purity even more.

Perhaps if we focused on preserving the kiss and seeing it as a gift rather than an expectation, the issues of premarital sex and the loss of virginity would naturally go away. I, for one, am praying that my children, at least, will see it that way. It is probably unrealistic, but it does not hurt to have noble and challenging goals to strive toward. It keeps you honest and alert, don't you think?

I believe it is good to teach our children how innocent gestures like kissing are connected to love, marriage, and virginity, and that there is meaning behind every action. Virginity is sacred and should be cherished. But it can't be unless we are willing to consider that all physical contact, including kissing, plays an important role in preserving it.

Worth the Wait

I know that in this day and age it is difficult to find someone who has not succumbed to the powerful and plentiful temptations of premarital sexual activity. But if you can manage to do it, saving yourself for marriage shows your future spouse the ultimate respect because of the very graphic nature of what marriage is: giving another person rights to your body. At a wedding ceremony, two persons exchange the rights to each other's bodies. What a beautiful gift it is to give this person your virginity along with those rights!

Many people do not understand how premarital sex relates to virginity. It's not about avoiding pregnancy (although that is important), nor about it being a sin (although that is also important), nor about it being hard to combat because of the human weakness of two people who are falling in love (although this is important to understand). At the heart of virginity is the right to express our sexuality. A consecrated individual's virginity is a vow to God which voluntarily, generously, and joyfully forfeits the right to give one's body to another person as a gift to God in consecrated life. Why? Because that individual will be married to God, and He will hold the rights to that person's body.

For those who feel they are called to marriage, their body is to be a gift to that one person they choose of their own free will, and with whom their sexuality will be expressed. It is a must that they use their bodies sacramentally in this divine design of their sexuality, which is meant to unify, procreate, and permanently bond. Every act of premarital intercourse is wrong primarily because it does not follow a freewill exchange of rights to each other's body. Therefore, neither one has a right to commit that sacred act.

Too many people are not able to save themselves for marriage. This does not mean they have lost their chance for a holy sacramental union. Although a person who has premarital sex is still capable of having a happy and holy marriage, that person has lost the chance to offer this gift of self to God and their future spouse. This is very sad. I pray that more singles will realize how tragic it is to give up one's virginity for temporary physical pleasure that cannot guarantee future happiness, and how significant it is to give that virginity to the person to whom they pledge their life.

CHAPTER FIVE

B e c o m e Charitable

DO YOU EVER FEEL THAT for someone to date you they would have to consider you a real charity case? I hope that does not describe your feelings about anyone who might ask you out. And to ask someone out because you pity him or her is not what it means to become charitable.

You are not a charity case. You are a beautiful, wonderful, special child of God, capable of sharing the person you are with other human beings. You have the gift of love, and you desire to share it with someone. That is a very real and powerful truth about you.

Did you know that this gift of love you have and desire to share is charity?

Defining Charity

No one can have love to give without having God to give, because God is love. Whether we are aware of it or not, when we share love with another person, we share God. Love that reaches out of the self toward another person is not of human origin. God has created each of us as capable vehicles of His love to transmit throughout the world.

To have the desire to share love with another person, therefore, comes from God. He inspires the heart and mind to take what He has given to the individual and bring it to another person. The desire to love is a gift, but it is also a necessity. Giving love to others is the only way to grow in charity, become a better person, and grow closer to God.

We are born with original sin, which inclines us to be self-centered. Though original sin is removed at baptism, the effects remain, making a lifelong struggle against selfishness. The remedy for selfishness is charity, which takes the focus off of us and shifts it onto others. You could define charity as love that sacrifices our own wants and makes becomes greater through giving to others.

Charity acts on behalf of others because of who they are, not because of what they need or whether they are deserving. A person might be in need, and we might provide for their need, but this can be done without charity. Charity starts with the dignity of the person, recognizing that he or she is a child of God, made in His image and likeness and thus lovable. Love of God is the motive, and love of neighbor follows. From there you can take care of a need, give what is asked for, give something beneficial even though it was not asked for, spend time, lend an ear, and so on. Love also might be shown by depriving a person of something he or she should not have.

Love is God, and we love for God's sake those whom God brings into our lives, those the Holy Spirit inspires us to love. Therefore, charity is a mission to bring God's love to others, despite our own needs or wants. In fact, the deepest expression of charity is when it involves suffering as we love another. The two pennies of the widow in the Gospel (see Luke 21:1–3) comes to mind. She gave all she had, and Our Lord said the man who gave one-third of his wealth was not as charitable.

It often hurts to be charitable. We are attached to our money and to our material things. We treasure our time and are inconvenienced when we have to spend it doing something we prefer not to do. We are bothered by people we do not care for, our enemies, or even friends we just don't want take the time to see.

We are called to become more charitable by loving others enough to put their needs before our own. But the joy we have in loving God in the charity we live lightens burdens and softens pain. Therefore, by God's love (grace), we are able to share money, material things, and time. And we are able to love our family, friends, strangers, those who bother us, and even our enemies. We give generously of ourselves to them all.

Generosity is a key aspect to charity. The more generous we are in the love we give to others, the more it hurts, and also the more grace we receive from God. Our spiritual life grows and expands in proportion to our generosity.

Dating couples need to witness the life of charity in each other as they date and seek to determine if they are meant to enter into Christian marriage together. They must be cautious of the romantic love that is more naturally the focus in dating and courtship. This love is about affection and feelings, and it is beautiful. But it is not charity. This love can put you on the road to charity, and it helps to motivate a couple to have charitable love for each other.

Charitable love for each other is sacrificial. How willing are you to make sacrifice for another person? Are there times when love hurts? There should be. A healthy, serious dating relationship should have both the romantic feelings associated with falling in love, as well as the proof of sacrificial love that gives even when it hurts or has no pleasant feeling accompanying it.

Charity involves the good things you have a natural right to but voluntarily sacrifice for another person. Sacrificing your good for someone else gives you something better than choosing to keep it for yourself.

This fundamentally applies to marriage itself. While single, you can do what you want whenever you want. In marriage, you have to share, compromise, and be of service to your spouse. This is mutual, of course, so you both benefit from sharing each other's love. The crosses and the blessings are all part of giving yourself to another for a lifetime.

It is a great act of charity to help another person enter into their vocation along with you and give them the opportunity to share the gift of love. You both love and are loved. You are each the recipient of the other's life of charity.

God is love. And you are love because of God in you. The love you share in marriage is a mutual charity that is very Trinitarian. God is Three Persons. Each Person *is* love. Love is communal; therefore, it is freely given to others. Marital love is a great witness of this love of the Father, Son, and Holy Spirit.

While you are single and dating, you live the life of charity through your dating experiences, as well as in all other aspects of your life. You can be sure you are called to extend charity, both in thought and in deed, to whoever God puts in your path on a daily basis. Becoming charitable is an excellent way to prepare for the great self-sacrificial gift of charity that is marital love.

The Peacemaker

Charitable love naturally calls us to a life of peace. The angel appeared to the shepherds on Christmas proclaiming the Good News with tidings of joy and peace to men of good will. Jesus appeared to the apostles after His resurrection, and the first thing He said was, "Peace be with you" (John 20:21).

It is no coincidence that after offering His peace, Jesus gave His apostles the power to forgive sins, which is fundamentally the power to restore peace to the soul. What a gift Catholics have in the sacrament of penance to have sins forgiven and peace restored.

The power to restore peace is available to all of us—not as priests do in the sacrament of penance, but by being peacemakers. Jesus said, "Blessed are the peacemakers, for they will be called children of God" (Matthew 5:9). Jesus loves peace. He puts great importance on it, because without peace, there is a vacancy of good that allows evil to infiltrate.

The devil is real, just as sin and evil are real. His mission is to lead souls away from God. Disrupt a person's internal peace, and the rest is easy. We are capable of just about anything once we have lost our interior peace. The devil tempts us to get caught up in the moment so we act without thinking while we have no peace.

Before you can be a peacemaker, you have to understand what peace is. Peace has to do with both the interior and exterior environment of a person." Interiorly, it is a state of being. Exteriorly, it is a condition for us to live our lives with others. Peace does not necessarily mean silence or calm. Families have various dynamics, and there can be peace even among a hectic or loud household. There might even be shouting matches at times, but family members find a way to resolve things. My own upbringing featured a large clan of Italians. They talked loud and yelled at each other, but they were laughing or kissing each other the next minute.

St. Augustine has what I think is the best definition of peace. He says that peace is the "tranquility of order."[2] An ordered life is a peaceful life. When disordered things are put back in order, there is a restoration of peace. To have resolve is to come to peace.

Interior order comes from Christ, Who offers His peace to us as a pure gift. We voluntarily forfeit this gift when we lose our peace or give someone else the power to take it away. Though all around us might fall apart and be at unrest, our internal peace can and should remain. This grace of Jesus comes from the ordered internal life of someone who enjoys friendship with God. Sin causes a disturbance in that friendship, and we are no longer tranquil. Sin disorders our soul and our very being. Confession and repentance put things back into order, and peace returns. This is the cycle of daily life for a sinner striving for sanctity. It is a daily struggle that Christ's peace stabilizes and orders.

The external order flows from the internal peace we maintain. As we are internally at peace, we are able to transmit that peace to others and into our external situations and experiences. We cannot help any external disorder if we lack internal peace. But assuming we are at peace, we can bring peace to those in our lives.

Peace is a gift to others that was first granted to us freely by Christ. We share this gift generously by being a source of peace to the people in our life.

Singles who are dating must find peace in each other if there is any hope of creating and growing in the friendship that makes for marital love. An ordered relationship creates a place for love to be founded and nurtured. What good is anything we have to offer someone in marriage if we cannot offer peace?

Without peace in a relationship, there is unrest and uncertainty, which cause anxiety about what might happen next. Peace ensures a freedom to be. The ability to relax around each other and be oneself is a wonderful quality in a couple's relationship. If you have to work hard at being something you are not just so you will have some semblance of peace, how good can the relationship be? This is not authentic peacemaking. To be a peacemaker does not mean losing yourself in the process. And it does not mean making sure there is no conflict, or the absence of anger. That would be a false peace.

Authentic peacemaking seeks to restore order in the relationship so there is freedom to be. Tranquility means that there is calmness, serenity, harmony. It means that both individuals involved are restored to order, not one person appeasing the other just to have the shouting stop.

A person who easily loses his or her peace and causes trouble is very unbecoming. It is a loss of love's way to lose peace. Without love we are nothing. Being able to make peace in a troubled situation, even when you are in the right, is a great act of charity. To become charitable is to become a peacemaker.

A Peaceful Family Environment Fosters Charity

To find love in another is to find peace. Your love together should be one that experiences the transmission of Christ's peace through each other. No matter what happens, you are always able to recover by the charity of the person you love. Only two people who love peace, who have good will in their heart, can create a home for each other which can help each of them recover their peace. It is a great act of charity to have this kind of love.

Two people who love peace are able to create a home for their children that will allow their children to grow into the persons God has called them to be. It is an ordered home with true freedom.

If you are dating someone who is easily disturbed or angered, who prolongs problems without a desire to see them quickly resolved, or who seems to like drama in their life, then you are dealing with someone who is not a peaceful person. A person who is not at peace with themselves will not actively provide a peaceful environment.

One of the most important examples of the Holy Family of Jesus, Mary, and Joseph is the way they lived a peaceful life, which allowed for a healthy family life.

Jesus had no need of baptism, yet He allowed himself to be baptized as an example to us. He had no need to be formed as a person by His earthly parents, yet He submitted Himself to them in all things. It is by this submission to Mary and Joseph that He was fully prepared for His mission of saving the world.

We start out as infants, completely at the mercy of our parents to form us into the persons we were created to be. Without good parenting, we are at risk of not becoming who we were meant to be, but rather some distorted version of that person.

Therefore, if an individual is neglected, abused, unloved, poorly educated, misguided, or many other things that fall under bad parenting, he or she does not turn out to be what society would call a "good person."

Parenting matters in the formation of every child to become a healthy, virtuous, civil adult of good character. The parents we have and the environment we grow up in play major roles in who we become as an adult. Thus, it is no small matter to choose a spouse who will make a good parent, and who desires to establish a home environment that will give children the best opportunity to become the people they are created to be by God. You should *be* this kind of person too, for this is the person your future spouse is seeking.

The Holy Family

The home of Jesus, Mary, and Joseph was a peaceful, harmonious home, full of joy and simplicity of life. It was a stable environment, where mutual love and respect was a priority. Jesus was taught normal things and guided by His mother and father. His human will was developed to confirm to God's will. There was no place for anger, aggression, or dominance of one over another in their home. Jesus was able to grow up with real freedom of self-discovery.

Jesus had two parents who were of one mind and direction. They both loved God, and their religion was central to their lives. The teachings of their religion governed their daily actions. They taught their son to love God and follow the teachings of their faith. Mary and Joseph were consistent and without controversy when it came to matters of importance. Today, a husband and wife should strive for this same kind of home life.

Finding someone who believes in peace and is a person of charity is vital to creating a happy, healthy home. It is critical to authentic love, which should always seek peace and resolve. A person of charity has the other's best interest in mind. Even if there are times of conflict, the end result should be a desire to make peace. The home, then, is where love and forgiveness are lived.

The environment of peace and charity produces well-adjusted children who can make the transition into adulthood with a firm sense of who they are, and who have the confidence to seek out what it is they are meant to do. They are free to become the persons they were created to be. Their parents did not try to control them in their development but guided them with the freedom to discover themselves.

The environment in which a couple raises their children influences who they become. It is concerning to see households where everyone is so busy, especially with parents who have their children constantly achieving and participating. Too often, an environment that is fast-paced and cluttered with activity, anxiety, pressure, and excessive entertainment can become counterproductive.

We do not know if Jesus was ever on the honor role or won awards in athletics. But we do know He led a humble, simple, and predictable life, obedient to Mary and Joseph. The message seems to be that what is important in the vocation of marriage and family life is simplicity—something very attainable for all. It is a serenity that comes from within, with God at the heart.

Above all, the Holy Family prayed. You cannot maintain charity and a sense of peace without a prayer life. Therefore, a couple should pray for each other, as well as *with* each other. Without this cornerstone, the entire structure falls. Those who believe in peace and are people of charity are definitely people of prayer. Always consider the prayer life of a person you think you could one day marry.

The peace, charity, and good will that was at the heart of the life of the Holy Family should be the priority of all who seek love, marriage, and family life.

The Rare Quality of Empathy

Charitable love is empathetic. Empathy is becoming a rare quality in people. Plenty of people are apathetic or sympathetic, but rare is the truly empathetic person.

Apathy is the all-too-common position of distance and detachment from concern for other people. It seeks to not get involved and feels nothing amidst the distresses and sufferings of others. There is no movement of the heart; apathetic persons are outside of people. They do not know love or charity, and they think only of themselves and their own concerns. Full of indifference, they walk by the downtrodden without a look or a care.

Sympathy, by contrast, is a firm movement of the heart toward another. It feels the pain of others and desires to help in some way. A sympathetic person is moved to pity and is willing to invest emotion, time, and action in service to those with whom they sympathize. Those who receive sympathy will feel a genuine care for their welfare. Those who sympathize want to do what is right. In sympathy, they walk by the downtrodden and perhaps give them money for some food and shelter.

Empathy, however, is when a person actually enters into the place of another, feeling what they feel, even dying with them if need be. Empathy picks up where sympathy leaves off, and enters further into the experience of the person. God became man in order to experience all that man experiences, and God knows what it's like to go through what we are going through. Those who receive empathy feel not only helped but loved. Charitable love exchanged provides an intimacy, a union, a bond, a fellowship, a connection. The empathic are moved in their heart to the point of pity, tears, joy, or some other deep emotion. Words spoken are sincere and comforting. The one so loved feels understood. There is true compassion, with a sharing in suffering.

To become charitable is to practice empathy. Marital love is empathetic, for it a mutual movement of hearts reaching out to love each other in such a way that they experience each other's joys and sufferings, and they grow together in deep union and compassion for one another. Charity shares in the suffering of another.

A Charitable You

Where charity and love prevail, there is God. Your dating life cannot be absent of charity if you are going to establish a foundation of true love that leads to marriage. Do you cultivate a spirit of sacrifice in your dating life? Are you a source of peace to each other? Are you building a friendship based on a love that is compassionate towards one another as much as it focuses on companionship and affection?

Charity is the proof of a Christ-centered love. Living charity frees you from selfishness, and provides the ultimate joy of giving love as God has loved you. Those you date need to see that you can give of yourself when it hurts, not just when it is convenient or easy. All you do should be motivated by your love for God, not by selfish motives.

In a word, those you date need to see a charitable you. It is the closest likeness to Christ you can hope to achieve. At least strive for it, and you will make progress. Utilize the peace that comes in the sacrament of Confession to be restored in charity. This is the love and the life your future spouse is seeking.

CHAPTER SIX

B e c o m e Merciful

WOULDN'T IT BE GREAT IF our loved ones always did the right thing? If that were realistic, the Lord would not have put such an emphasis on forgiveness. It is easy to love those who love you. In other words, it's easy to love when all is going well. It is the times when things are not going so well when our professed godliness, even our very Christianity, is challenged and put to the test.

Receiving the mercy of God is an essential aspect of our redemption and future share in the resurrection. God is merciful, and we should be so thankful that He is. Otherwise, we would be lost. As Christians, we know we also are called to be merciful, but we excuse ourselves from imitating God because we are only human. It would be great if we could be merciful, but God cannot possibly expect us be as merciful as He is, can He?

Yet isn't it hypocritical for us to benefit from the mercy of God while justifying ourselves for not being merciful to others? As Catholics, we have to study and become familiar with the corporal and spiritual works of mercy, and we are expected to live them.

For those who are dating, finding love and entering into marriage has everything to do with becoming merciful, though I am sure many give no thought to it. Let us reflect on some key aspects of what it means to become merciful and discover how this applies to your dating experiences and eventually your married life.

Mercy: A Sense of Home

"With the LORD there is mercy / and with him is plenteous redemption" (Psalm 130:7). Earlier in this psalm, in verse 3, we read the sobering words, "If you, O LORD, should mark iniquities, / Lord, who could stand?" In other words, if God keeps a record of our sins, who could ever make it to heaven?

None of us *wants* to sin, yet we do. We sin daily. God is merciful toward us first of all because He knows that without His mercy we are lost. We do not deserve His mercy, but He grants it freely. Our repentance and our desire to do better by God's grace shows God that we recognize our need for His mercy. Though we might commit the same sins over and over again, He continues to have mercy on us by forgiving the sins we acknowledge and confess and are truly sorry for.

I like to think of a good relationship that lasts the life of a marriage as a home. And this home, this relationship, must be built of material that can withstand the evil winds that attempt to destroy it. The idea of being home when you are together is the essence of love. This is why you feel you are home as long as you are with the person you love, no matter where you are, whether you are together in the same place or not. It is why you long to get back to that person when you are apart from them. You want to be home.

The foundation of this home is mercy and forgiveness. Our human condition is a fallen one, prone to sin and failure in our actions. We continually strive to be better individuals, but failure is part of life for all of us, and therefore all human relationships will be tested by actions that hurt us or those we love.

With love as home, these hurtful actions and failures have a place to be resolved because mercy is available. We are accepted and welcomed because we are loved. There, mercy shown to us when we are the guilty party frees us and makes reconciliation possible.

Isn't this ultimately what heaven will be like? Heaven is our only true and lasting home. This world is not our home. Yet, we get a taste of our true heavenly home through the people who love us. It is really Jesus Christ Himself who loves us through them. Our time on this earth is brief, but it provides us with the opportunity to experience this eternal home while in this world in order to help us be fashioned into the saints we are to become.

Our entire life on earth can be summed up this way: We are sinners trying to become saints. But all too often, we are expected to be saints at all times without much (if any) room for failure. Many of us who are dating and seeking a suitable partner for marriage seem to come up short, because we do not want to marry someone who can potentially hurt us. Therefore, we are quick to dismiss someone for their flaws, their past, or other ways we determine them to be damaged because we see these things as a potential threat to having a hurt-free marriage.

God, of course, is the only one who can fulfill this high expectation. God is pure love and incapable of anything that is not good for us. Yet we still foolishly pursue finding in another person what only God can give. God is home. With Him you find complete safety, security, warmth, welcome, comfort and peace. With human beings, not so much.

However, we are called to be like God, and we are provided with the grace to do so. Unfortunately, I think too many take this call to mean that we must never sin. It is clear that God is realistic about us and knows that we can and will sin, or else He would never have instituted the beautiful sacrament of reconciliation. When we go to confession, our sins are obliterated and we are given a clean slate.

God is offended when we sin, and our relationship with Him is negatively affected. He wants us to live virtuous lives, but He knows we are sinners, so He is always ready to forgive and show mercy. It's not because we deserve it, but because His love is most importantly displayed for us when we are at our worst. We deserve our relationship with Him to end due to our sin, but He chooses instead to show mercy.

Shouldn't we have this same approach to others? It is natural that we too are offended by those who offend or hurt us and our relationship negatively affected. But, like God, we can provide mercy to all who wrong us. This aspect of being like God, being merciful to others, is much more attainable to us than living without sin.

Mercy is at the heart of the law of love. Essentially, God loves us so much that He welcomes us home when we have lived foolishly and want to return home, just like the Prodigal Son.

Home is where the heart is. But more specifically, home is where the Heart of Christ is. As we give our heart to the Heart of Christ, we live a love that makes us an attractive, welcoming, home.

In modern dating, there is so much focus put on finding someone who gives pleasure, makes you feel good, and won't hurt you. This causes even good Catholics a lot of trouble when it comes to making a wise choice for marriage. People fall in love with this focus, and it clouds their mind.

While in this cloud, they can lose sight of what they really are seeking, which is to find a home. We all want a place where we can be ourselves and not have to worry about the inevitable moments of failure and sin. We want to find that kind of love in the person we desire to give ourselves to.

Because it is a fundamental reality in every person to desire God, Who created us for Himself, all pursuits of a home in this life are connected to the natural desire to seek God, and they can never be completely satisfied until we are in our eternal home in heaven with God.

As we live the attributes of that eternal home, which is mercy, we can meditate on the words of Psalm 130, "With the Lord, there is mercy and fullness of redemption." Where it says "the Lord," insert your own name and consider with Jesus how true this is when it comes to your dealings with others. Are you home to the one you love?

The Jesus Environment

We all want to be loved, which is really the longing to meet God in others. To be loved is to experience the Heart of Christ.

The first call of the Christian is to love, to live that Heart of Christ, to be merciful. "What would Jesus do?" is sadly not a question we Christians are anxious to seriously ask. When it comes to dating and marital love, this is even more of a concern.

So what *would* Jesus do? Jesus always, without fail, was receptive to anyone who desired to change their ways and have friendship with God. Sinners, adulterers, and tax collectors alike all found open and welcoming arms in Jesus. I call this the Jesus environment, and it is our example of how to live mercy.

When you are falling in love, you begin to develop a dependency on the other person for your happiness. It is natural. The more you love someone, the more it hurts when they fail you. The law of love demands that there be forgiveness, if there is a sincere desire to be forgiven and a resolve not to hurt you again.

If Jesus were sitting next to you, you would have no trouble disclosing every detail about what you did and your regrets. Jesus, in all His mercy, would say something like, "It's not beyond any human being to do such things," with the kindest voice and in such a welcoming way. You would share what you did and ask forgiveness because you feel completely safe with him. The environment that Jesus provides is a safe, homey one. There is nothing that can happen that is unforgivable. His mercy endures forever.

As you date someone and develop a relationship, love and the desire to marry grow stronger. That safe and homey environment should be present, cultivated, and established. The more it is established, the safer you feel about being yourself, sharing yourself, and even sharing your faults, weaknesses, and sins. When you fall, you recover quickly because the mercy of your loved one is always there.

A cynical person might say that this is a recipe for disaster because eventually the other person will take advantage, knowing that mercy is waiting for them no matter what. This discounts the notion that justice for actions that must be tended to within any relationship, not to mention the emotional pain that needs healing. Though one might be merciful, they also can be hurt and must heal.

Starting with mercy is best because it says that no matter what has happened, you love each other, you are safe, and you can get through anything. If the one who hurts you does not have a sense of Jesus's environment of mercy, he or she will have fear about what has happened. This fear can keep your loved one from doing what is necessary to remedy the problem, which can further hurt the relationship.

How many of us have been in relationships where we felt we could not confess something we did or feared disclosing parts or all of what happened? This is not normal in a healthy relationship. True friends love each other regardless of what they do. When you wrong a true friend, your friend's mercy is waiting. It might take time to reestablish the level of friendship and trust again, but your friend will not abandon you, physically or emotionally.

Being merciful is also incredibly attractive. It is rare to find someone who sees you the way Jesus does. People tend to react with anger or some other negative reaction first, instead of with mercy. This is unbecoming. When we do something wrong that we regret, it is hard enough to face within ourselves. When we have to face the one we love, knowing we have hurt them, it can be terrifying. How incredible it is if the first hurtful experience with the one you love is a merciful experience! Your loved one doesn't react negatively. He or she does not scream or cry or throw a fit. They don't storm out.

Instead, that person calmly looks at you as you share what you have done. Perhaps he or she takes your hand, or hugs you, or softly speaks. Your loved one first reminds you that you are safe and home. You are able to realize that nothing you have done is something your loved one could not have done as well; you are not unforgivable, irredeemable, or unloved.

People do a lot of stupid things. Most of it stems from bad habits they have developed. All of it is due to our weak human nature. It is way too easy to pass judgment on others as you are dating, and way too convenient to say that this is not *the one*. For many individuals, it is entirely too difficult to trust those they date enough to cut them slack, give them a pass, be merciful. The risk of being taken advantage of is too great.

As Catholics, we must be merciful. We must cut others slack. We must give others a pass. We can help others feel safe to be themselves.

We must work at true friendship. Love is kind and merciful. If you want love in your life, it has to start with you.

The only way for there to be real progress is if the one who offends you first feels safe enough to fail. How many times did the disciples Jesus loved fail Him?

I cannot stress this enough. There are so many relationships where one or both live in fear of how the other will react if the other one blows it or messes up. What this means is that there are way too many people seeking love who are not encountering the mercy of Jesus Christ in the person they are dating. Instead, their relationship is tainted by fears of what the other might do or say because of their shortcomings. What kind of relationship is that? Is this the kind of relationship we have with Jesus?

The Bible tells us that love casts out all fear (see 1 John 4:18). We never have to be afraid with Jesus because He is our home. We feel safe with Him. We can tell Him anything and know that He will forgive us and share grace with us that helps us be better.

You most certainly are forgivable and redeemable. You are not your sins. You do sinful things, but that is not who you are. It is important to feel safe enough to hurt the one you love, trusting in their mercy first, and preparing to fulfill justice in the situation second. You are not a terrible person because you feel too afraid to talk to the person you are in love with. A true friendship will naturally draw out the desire to share everything because you feel safe and comfortable in that person's love.

This is the essence of healthy marital love. Singles need to practice providing the Jesus environment of mercy for those they date. It is the first priority, since married life primarily requires a safe, homey environment where forgiveness can be asked for and applied when spouses hurt one another. If you fear talking to the person you are dating or have experienced negative reactions as a result of trying to talk to them, and if you do not feel comfortable sharing your faults or wrongdoings with that person, this is a serious problem that must be remedied if your relationship is to thrive.

There will always be problems. Loved ones will fail you. Your first call in all situations is to be merciful, maintaining a strong sense that only God will never let you down. In fact, if you expect failure in others, you will live more peacefully.

Forgive and Forget

Forgiveness: This is a powerful word that is losing its meaning in our culture. We say, "Please forgive me," and "I forgive you," but do we really mean it? It's getting to the point where even saying these phrases is insulting, because so often there is no true repentance or sorrow on the part of the one who asked forgiveness, and no sincere commitment to forgive and forget about the offense by the offended party.

Many struggle with the "and forget" part, believing it is too much to ask. They think that if they forget about the offense, it gives the offender license to do it again. Forgiveness does not mean forcing yourself to not remember wrongs done to you. Maybe you cannot help remembering what was done, but it is your responsibility to at least forgive with the intention of not bringing that offense up again.

Often you might be tempted to use a past offense as a weapon against the person. If the offender was sincerely sorry for what he or she did, your forgiveness is a pledge to never use that offense against them again. But you might ask, "What if the same thing happens again, or what if it keeps happening?" Well, from the Christian standpoint, you address the repeated offense as if it were the first time it has happened.

Thankfully, this is how God works with us. When we are forgiven by the priest in confession, God has no recollection of that offense any longer. If we repeat the same sin, He does not have a running tally of how many times we did it and how many times He has had to forgive it. We disobey, choosing to disrupt our relationship with Him, and then we ask forgiveness and are restored to friendship with Him.

However, God has the benefit of living with two other Divine Persons. Since we are human, there is only so much we can take, and we are not always so ready or able to get past being offended. This is where we must address the matter of repeated offenses in the context of potential harm to ourselves, others in the house, or to the offending person themselves. But we are still called by Christ to forgive and forget, without allowing the hurt to penetrate and affect our being. It is hard not to take things personally, which is what makes forgiveness so powerful and necessary for any love relationship to grow.

If you cannot forget the offense as part of your forgiveness, then the offense continues to harm your person, making you part of the ongoing problem by how it affects you. Forgiveness brings healing to *both* parties. Too often, not forgetting an offense makes it part of you. The next time you are offended by someone's actions, that unforgotten offense plays a role in how you approach forgiveness in the present.

You really can't afford *not* to forget offenses when you forgive. You have no choice but to trust that person if forgiveness is to be authentic. You are too valuable to allow another person's offense to do permanent damage to you. All kinds of psychological problems develop when we do not let go of past hurts, and it affects our ability to forgive in the future.

Again, prudence dictates that you address repeated offenses in a manner appropriate to helping both parties involved, but that requires a detachment from taking the offense so personally that you internalize it and make it part of you.

Extend Mercy to Others

We must not let people mistreat us in any way that is contrary to our human dignity. Just because we forgive them does not mean they should always expect forgiveness. But, at the same time, we shouldn't mistreat someone we have forgiven just because we don't like what they did to us.

You might say, "Well, I forgive them, but that doesn't mean I have to be around them anymore." Oh no? Do you really believe that? That might be true depending on the situation, but often the person we must forgive is someone we are bound to in some way. It can be the path of least resistance to decide you cannot be around this person, but maybe the real truth is that you just don't want to deal with it anymore.

No relationship is affected more seriously by a lack of forgiveness than marriage, specifically because of the promises made to each other. The nature of marriage requires a heroic forgiveness at times. Anger and harbored resentment for past offenses that were not forgotten contribute to the feeling of being fed up, of reaching the end of one's rope. This needs to be considered.

Our Lord calls us to forgive others. We cannot forgive as the Lord commands us to unless we are merciful. To forgive someone requires showing mercy. Maybe the person does not deserve your forgiveness, but he or she needs you to be merciful and forgiving anyway. It takes humility to be merciful, because when you see yourself as God sees you and realize how merciful He has been to you, this fosters a humility in you that allows you to deal with others in the same manner.

How easily we make excuses for our lack of true forgiveness! How self-righteous and cruel it is to say, "I forgive you, but I am done with you," when the other person shows a sincere desire to make things right.

Is it not God who brings a person into our life? Are we arrogant enough to think that *we* control having someone in our life? Do we really have a right to be absolutely done with someone, even if they have hurt us many times, or for many years?

The point is, forgiveness involves mercy and demands our charity. Forgiveness is an act of God, which we are not capable of by ourselves. It is not in our nature as human beings to forgive; only God can enable us to truly forgive. We should pray daily for the grace to forgive and show mercy.

To cut someone out of your life because you have had enough is dangerous. It is understandable that the level of hurt inflicted by someone you love can drain you and harm you to the point of feeling broken. And if you have lost the feeling of love for the person, it makes it that much easier to justify ending the relationship. You just want to get away from it. And of course there are legitimate reasons to end a relationship with someone who is destructive, abusive, or even dangerous. In those circumstances, forgiveness requires letting go and moving forward.

But in many situations that lead to a severed relationship, including divorce, a lack of forgiveness is the root problem, and there is no mercy that allows for reconciliation. Someone might believe it will take too long and he or she does not want to risk wasting more time. Ironically, true forgiveness coupled with true repentance often produces very quick results.

Mercy involves giving someone the grace they do not deserve. God shows mercy to us because of His kindness and generosity, not because we deserve it. In turn, we respond to God's loving mercy with a true spirit of repentance. In like manner, we show mercy out of kindness and generosity. Forgiveness comes in time, but mercy is the gateway to the beginnings of reconciliation.

It might be too difficult to forgive someone when they first ask for forgiveness. But the road to forgiveness has to start somewhere, and it always starts with the kind gesture of mercy. Mercy allows the offender back into our heart so that the work of repentance and reconciliation can begin.

If you find that you just cannot forgive someone, or you forgive without a willingness to reconcile, it is time for you to reevaluate your spiritual life. If you can't do it, you can't do it. Just realize it is just as much your problem as it is the one you cannot forgive. That way you will not sow further seeds of resentment and animosity as you move forward in your life.

I encourage you to become a forgiving person. Practice forgiveness by conscientiously being merciful to people, especially those who you think do not deserve it. This requires a spirit of kindness and generosity. Meditate often on how merciful God has been to you, and how others have shown you mercy for things you have done in your past.

A Safe, Welcoming Place

Can you think of someone in particular who has forgiven you or shown you mercy in such a way that made you feel better about yourself and helped you take a positive step forward in your life?

The people in our lives that we love and bond with are God-given for a reason. Though some may end by necessity, too many relationships end because of a lack of true forgiveness. The people in our lives are gifts. They should not be disposed of too readily or without absolute necessity. Usually, there is nothing that a little forgiveness and mercy cannot fix.

God calls all of us to imitate His kindness, His benevolence, and His healing power through the gift of mercy. It is a magnificent gift to bring to your spouse on your wedding day and throughout your married life. Because human beings fail each other, your mercy is a warm and welcoming place where your spouse knows he or she is always accepted and loved, even when your spouse feels undeserving.

Make the one you love feel safe. Become merciful and forgive, for you never know when you will need such kindness and mercy from someone you have offended.

CHAPTER SEVEN

B e c o m e Detached

LOVE BETWEEN A MAN AND a woman is one of the most beautiful things in the world. But what happens when your love for another person becomes the most important thing in your life?

There is nothing more natural than wanting to be loved. We need it. We need it from our parents and family as we grow up, and we need it as we interact socially as adults. We all have a fundamental desire to be loved by at least one person who knows us and fulfills our every personal need. With marital love, there is the additional need to be physically intimate as an expression of love.

Though the need to be loved emotionally, physically, and spiritually is completely natural, it also poses a danger: becoming overly attached to each other.

What is wrong with being attached to someone you love? Doesn't attachment come with the territory? Yes...and no. Yes, you become attached to someone you love in a way that compels a real commitment to that person, one that is not easily broken. To call someone a friend assumes a dedication to that person because of who they are and your decision to love them.

For those who have experienced attachment to someone in a love that lasts a lifetime, there is a fulfillment in this world that is a gift.

Not many find it. The reality is that human relationships can end, regardless of the intention to love each other for life no matter what. Friendships fail, engagements are broken, and marriages end in separation and divorce.

When you are in a serious relationship, you assume it will never die. No couple enters into a marriage thinking anything other than that they are going to make it until death. But when there is an end to a relationship, there is often a certain level of death inside, also known as a broken heart.

The Dangers of Attachment

Everyone experiences love uniquely. Therefore, no one can really know how another person will grow in love or deal with the end of love. No matter how love is handled, whether in good times or bad, attachment to a person is the main reason for the things we do in the name of love.

In this sense, attachment is dangerous. When you rely too much on another person's love, you may go too far and deify that person. In other words, you just might have made this person your god. This person is now the pinnacle of your existence, with nothing or no one above them.

To assign another human being that much importance in your life is to set yourself up for disaster. You have put another human being on a pedestal, where they do not belong, nor can they remain.

Has this happened to you? In one sense, though, when you are in love, how can you help it? You love someone so intensely, so deeply, so completely, that you cannot imagine life without them. This is beautiful, and there is nothing wrong with it. But you have to pay attention if you begin to feel you might not be able to live without that person.

Life is a gift from God. It is God who is your God, the primary focus of your affection. He made you out of nothing. He loves you more than any human being could possibly love you. He desires you to be with Him for all eternity, providing you with His love and grace throughout your life in order to accomplish this purpose.

Who in this world could be more important than God? Who has a right to your love above your Creator and Father in Heaven? You might emphatically tell me, "No one!" and mean it. I believe you. Why shouldn't I? I think everyone who believes in God wants to believe that they love Him above all else.

But in practice all of us are susceptible to self-deception when it comes to the place of God in our lives versus the place of our husband/wife, boyfriend/girlfriend, fiancé(e), best friend, parent, sibling, and so on. Our affection toward certain human beings we love is powerful. And the power of love shared by two human beings has a way of influencing the place of God. Thus another person ends up replacing the Divine Person as the one we love most.

Have you ever broken down and cried when you committed a sin or during confession? It is not all that common. But many tears are shed when a spouse dies or the person you date breaks up with you. It is painful to suffer the loss of human love, but somehow it does not seem as painful to suffer the loss of friendship with God through sin.

This is not proof that we do not love God above all, but it should make us think. And we should continually examine our consciences to make sure we haven't put anything or anyone else before God.

What happens on the inside is very telling, and we should pay attention to it. We can ask ourselves questions like: Does the love I have for another make me think, do, or feel something that is not in accordance with God's will? Are my reactions and emotions toward a person I love out of context to God's plan or the teachings of the Church?

If we are honest about our examination and do it in the light of Jesus Christ, we just might discover that we have an inappropriate attachment to someone. What would make it inappropriate? If the love we have for that person influences us to think or act in a way that is contrary to God's will and the natural order created by God, it indicates that something is out of balance. Another warning sign is if we do something associated with that loved one with a selfish motive, rather than out of love for God.

Jesus said, "If you love me, keep my commandments" (John 14:15), "Love one another even as I have loved you" (John 13:34), and "Greater love has no man than this, that a man lay down his life for his friends" (John 15:13). Obeying God, serving others, putting others' needs before our own, sacrificing for another's sake even to the point of death these are ways that show we love God above any human person.

Worship One God Only

You must learn detachment. The person you date and may eventually marry already has a God, and so do you. You are meant to worship only the one true God, not each other. Your loved one needs a partner, a helpmate, and a companion to share love and to help one another on the path toward the God you mutually worship. Detach from the one you love just enough to ensure that you don't lose yourself and that your priorities are straight if for some reason you are without that person.

God and His love can never be lost to us. God alone quenches love's thirst. Human beings can only love as they are living Christ's love. Human love fails. Human affection is not to be preferred over doing God's will. Love God first, and human love will flow proportionally and without contradiction to the love of God.

Enjoy the human love God provides in your life. But take your human relationships off that pedestal. That way of thinking is too unstable for them and too dangerous for you. Never expect any human being to fulfill your desire for love. Only God can do that.

Human love lures the heart, but God's love fully captures. Many quote St. Augustine, and for good reason: "Our hearts were made for Thee, O God, and they are restless until they rest in Thee." Entrust and share your heart to those you love, but know that only God can love completely and without fail.

Detachment From Creatures

Many saints wrote about detachment from all creatures as being necessary if we are to have union with God.

"Creatures": Does this mean spiders, alligators, and rats? Because those are creatures I think all of us are happily willing to detach from them. No, here the term *creatures* refers to the entire created world, everything external that we see. This includes animals, fish, insects, flowers, the forest, and even people. But it also includes food, clothes, electronic devices, our house, our bed, etc. These get the name *creature comforts* for a reason.

Everything material comes from the external world and affects our interior life. As we are inordinately attached to material things, our ability to develop in the spiritual life is impaired. The external world is a gift of God. All that God has created is good. God's gifts of imagination and invention allow man to use God's natural resources creatively, and this is also good.

Music is wonderful and ennobling. Listening to music is a positive form of recreation. But when music distracts the soul from God, whether in content or by the unreasonable amount of time experienced, it is no longer just innocent recreation. I was sitting behind a family at midnight Mass one Christmas, and the two teenage children were wearing earbuds. They were listening to their MP3 players while at Mass.

Life is full of distractions from the material world. And the attachments we develop are ever so subtle. They can even be things that seem holy and godly. Who would see anything wrong with a woman volunteering at the local nursing home three times per week? However, if her family needs her care at home those nights, there is a problem with volunteering.

My grandparents stopped going to Mass when the changes took place after the Second Vatican Council. They were attached to the Latin and all the externals that surrounded the Mass instead of the reality of holy sacrifice of Jesus Christ at the altar. Somewhere along the line, the rituals of the Mass became too essential to lose and were required for their attendance.

Though good in and of itself, anything external and material can be used to our detriment. When we voluntarily permit things to have more importance than they should, to the point of distraction away from God, they can become problematic.

And of course, detachment from creatures includes detachment from human beings. Without detachment from all creation, we cannot love God as the first commandment requires us with our whole heart, mind, body, and soul.

No person in this world is meant to replace God as first and foremost in our life in any way or for any reason. This is a difficult challenge, because we all love the comforts of life, the fun things to do, the people we like to be with. Life is beautiful, and things and people in life are important and essential to enhancing us as persons and fostering positive growth. But when we become distracted from God because of them, they become counterproductive.

The more comfortable we become in our life, the harder it gets to part with or give up things. Consider St. Peter who was warming himself by the fire as the Lord was on trial. When confronted with accusations that he was one of Jesus's disciples, he denied Him three times. He was not detached enough from the comforts of his life to be ready to stand up for what was right.

Are you ready to give witness to your Christianity publicly? Detachment from creatures while growing closer to the Lord conditions you to be able to do just that. Otherwise, your profession of faith is in word and desire only. You are not genuinely ready or able to love God over the things and people you love or enjoy.

It is a great service to those you date to determine what material things you are attached to and if you would choose any of them before choosing Christ, because your future spouse is looking for someone who can live out the demands of marriage with the ability to prioritize and adjust. Life is full of surprises. Unemployment, illness, pregnancy, death, financial changes, relocation—the possibilities are endless. A healthy level of detachment enables you to take these changes in stride and adapt to any situation.

After God, your spouse and children should be the highest priorities in your life. Choosing the Lord first and prioritizing the things of this world is what enables you to be a source of comfort and strength for your spouse in all that life brings your way. The practice of detachment from creatures while you are still single conditions you for an easier transition into marriage, as this is a source of comfort and strength.

Detachment From Your Own Will

There is a scene in the Gospels in which a leper approaches Jesus, asking to be clean and saying that Jesus can do it if he wills it. We are told that Jesus took pity on the leper and simply said, "I do will it." And God's will was done (see Matthew 8:2–3).

We all have a will that we are quite fond of and do not particularly care to have disrupted by the will of another. We also secretly struggle with God's will when it goes against our will, even though we are obliged to publicly profess we want God's will in our life.

The love of our will reveals what we desire and also what we decide to act on. This is important. It's not just what we desire, but what we decide to act on. The way we think things should go and how we think people should be, the plans we have, the ideas we come up with, and what we want these are aspects of our desire. But our will includes these things as well as the decision to act on them, whether we actually execute that will or not.

We see the world a certain way. It is our world, and everything should revolve around it. This is known as self-centeredness. To be self-centered is to be selfish. We are driven by what we want, and we employ our will to act on our wants. It is very much like the willfulness we had as a child—only as adults, we are better at masking it.

This is not to say that the things you want are wrong. Like everything else about you, your will is a gift of God and part of how you are designed to function. But, like everything else about you, your will is not meant to be self-governing. That is why you must not let your will act on everything you want. Making a good and wise decision is the function of your will.

You might say to someone, "I'll take you to dinner tonight," and so you do. You willed it and followed through. Or you might ask, "Will you marry me?" and your girlfriend says yes of her own free will. But at some point she might break it off, thus not following through with her original intent. Something changed her mind, and she is no longer willing to marry you.

Therefore, your will is only beneficial to you insofar as you are able to control it to execute everything you want and desire. Obviously you cannot will everything you want, but you must strive to will everything that is right and just and of the highest good. That does not always include what you want. Acts of charity are very often the doing of what is right for someone else at the expense of doing what you wanted.

- I want to stay in bed and sleep longer, but I *will* get up and go to Mass.
- I want to go out with my friends, but I *will* stay home and take care of my sick mother.
- I love you very much and do not want to lose you, but I *will* not see you again due to your pornography addiction.

We can will something, but we cannot go against another's will. We cannot control the situation. This explains why we get upset, disturbed, frustrated, impatient, annoyed, etc.

- I want that crying child to stop so I can hear the television, but the child will not.
- I wanted this new job very badly, but they hired someone else.
- I want to go out with him, but he will not ask me out.
- I want to marry her, but she said no.

When you will something and it does not happen, it is a test, not a condemnation. You can't always get what you want. You also can't always execute your will. Your will is not law. Detachment from your will is a detachment from your own plans and expectations, and it leads to true freedom.

Your plans may change despite what you want. What you must will (decide) is not what you wanted, but what is best. Detachment from your will, therefore, is detachment from yourself as an authority and requires a submission to a higher good. God's providence governs each of our lives, and His will must be done, not our own. The more knowledgeable we are of God's authority, the more capable we are of aligning our will with His.

Willing the Will of God

Jesus Christ is the authority of God. To follow Jesus is to live God's authority. To obey the teachings of Jesus Christ that come to us through His teaching authority on earth—the Catholic Church— is to live the will of God in our lives.

Are we *will*ing to seek out the truth: what is right and wrong, what is ethical, what is moral, what is the higher good, what is best for others? Our will should want to be aligned with God's will. What does God want? That should be what we want, and that should influence what we decide to do.

Learn all that God has made available to you. Study the life of Jesus, the Scriptures, and especially the *Catechism of the Catholic Church*. Read about the lives of the saints. Study the writings of those who represent official teachings of Christ's established Church. It gets much easier to detach from your own will and adhere to God's will as you learn and practice what you learn. You will then get in the habit of obeying God's will.

A famous part of a wedding ceremony is when the couple exchanges their vows by saying, "I do." The words should actually be "I will."

They really mean the same thing, but when you think about the will this way, it might add more meaning to the vows if you say, "I will."

Poverty of Spirit—Spiritual Riches

I hope you come away from this chapter knowing that the goal of detachment is union with God. The saints practiced detachment because union with God is impossible without it.

It is fitting to conclude this chapter by pointing out the first beatitude: "Blessed are the poor in spirit, for theirs is the kingdom of heaven" (see Matthew 5:3). Poverty of spirit means that you reside in the kingdom of heaven, even here on earth. How is this possible while in this world? With the eyes of faith and the grace of detachment. Growth in faith and grace are benefits souls that are disposed to God receive. How disposed are you to receive God's grace and grow in faith? The only way to answer that is to determine how poor you are.

Those who live in extreme poverty know what it's like to be detached. They basically have nothing, so there is nothing to be attached to. In a sense, the poor have it easier than most of us when it comes to detachment. But this kind of poverty merely relates to material things. It is one thing to be so poor that you suffer from a lack of creature comforts, but what about a poverty of love?

God does not require us to live in material poverty in order to love Him and our neighbor as we are called to do. Those of moderate means as well as the wealthy have just as much access to the kingdom of heaven as the poor. The point is not economic or social status; it's about the heart, the spiritual life.

No matter what our financial situation or social class, Jesus Christ calls us to poverty of spirit. Everything we have is at the service of God. This includes people in our life, and it especially includes a spouse and any children that come from the marriage. All things are gifts from God, and we are stewards of them.

Being poor in spirit means that nothing is really ours. Doesn't that change the way we look at dating? Too many singles have the notion that they are on a hunt to acquire a prize that is for their personal delight, never completely realizing that they are not detached from all that is motivating them toward this objective approach to love and marriage.

The poor in spirit will inherit the kingdom of heaven. The kingdom of heaven literally is theirs! To be open to someone and love them for God's sake is to be poor in spirit when it comes to marital love. You will recognize God in this person, your life with this person will be lived in the kingdom of heaven, and the sufferings you share with this person will be transformed. As we are detached, we know ourselves to be citizens of the heavenly kingdom. We are no longer attached to things of the world, which are passing. The more we are detached from the kingdom of this world, the more open we are to things of the kingdom of God. You cannot get closer to God without improving your allegiance. Having attachment to people and things of this world with too much loyalty can prevent a defense for your most important ally, the kingdom of heaven, when a decision to choose is called for. As we seek the riches of the kingdom of God more and more, we act accordingly, and we become poorer for all that is of this world. We grow in faith and grace.

This is why you can be very close to someone you love but still grow closer to God. The person is not the end goal of love, but a vehicle from which the love of God flows. And when someone we love fails us or perhaps is no longer with us, we are still focused on God, Who has allowed it, even as we struggle on the human level. Everything of this world is passing away. To be rich in this world with shared marital love is actually a personal poverty, because the person you love and the love you share are not for you to cling to but to give away. True love in relationships is always about giving love away to the extent of total poverty.

Detachment Is a Way of Life

To be detached is to spiritualize all things, seeing everything and everyone as being a gift from God, for God's purposes. It is recognizing our responsibility and role as coworkers with God. As we spiritualize things, we detach from being possessive of them.

If your spouse wrongs you, detachment allows you to accept the wrong as being permitted by God for some good in God's plan, and then proceed to address the situation accordingly. If your spouse dies, and after a normal period of grieving you still feel completely alone, useless, and without a will to go on, it reveals an inappropriate attachment to the person. Instead, with poverty of spirit, you mourn the death of your loved one while maintaining a steady trust in God's plan and God's love. Though a person might abandon you, God never will.

Those who are detached are content. They embrace simplicity. They are happy with what they have, and they are not overly ambitious, grasping for more. They are just as happy to have more as to have less, as long as it is all in accordance with God's will.

How detached are you from everything that comforts you, that you enjoy, that you love? Do these things distract you from God or lead you closer to Him? Be honest. Detachment is a way of life, and attachments can be subtle. Take the time to prayerfully seek out what you need to detach from, and enjoy the freedom you will experience.

Dating can be a distraction. Detach from the common, worldly notions of dating, and approach those you date with poverty of spirit.

Be open to God, detached from your will, and let God's will be done. Let detachment condition the eyes of your mind and heart. You will live in the kingdom of God more and more, and your decisions about love and marriage will become clearer.

CHAPTER EIGHT

B e c o m e Self-Aware

EACH OF US IS BROKEN in some way and to some degree. It is necessary for you to be aware of your own brokenness in order to take steps toward becoming a better, healthier individual.

It is important that a person you enter into a dating relationship with knows about any issues you might have and sees that you are dealing with them. If you have never addressed certain problems or are not healing from them, this is huge disservice to the person you are dating. These things need to be faced and discussed.

Let us take a general look at some of the more common areas each of us should become aware of as they apply to love, dating, and marriage.

Deal With Your Upbringing

First, you have to start with your upbringing. How you were raised has so much to do with who you are as an adult, and it affects your future married life more than you might think.

In marriage preparation, this exploration into the upbringing of the two individuals is covered in a section called "Family of Origin." Each individual's young life, the roles and involvement of parents and siblings, school experiences, the social environment, and any significant events that might have had an impact on each person's formation are considered in light of the person each one has become and will be giving to each other in marriage.

This is not a therapy session, but rather a general exploration of the way one was raised, and it is meant to give some insight into what each individual experienced as family life. It is likely that patterns of spousal interaction, the roles of husband and father, and parenting styles will be repeated in one's future marriage. Knowledge of one's own upbringing should be coupled with a general knowledge about what constitutes a healthy upbringing and learning about objective principles for being a good spouse and parent for comparison.

You are who you are because of your upbringing, whether you like it or not. You do not have to have had the perfect parents or family life to qualify for a successful marriage. But growing up in a dysfunctional family does increase the chances that your own marriage could be rocky. The fact is that no one has the perfect upbringing, and everyone is at least a little damaged by the way they grew up. How you address your upbringing is what really determines your future married life.

It has been said that you do not marry an individual, you marry a whole family. There is a lot of truth to this. You want to make sure you learn from your upbringing and can share these things honestly and openly within your dating relationships. Every family is different. No matter who you date, that person will have had a different upbringing than you. It's good to find someone who can relate to your past and accept it. Romantic love is wonderful, but those feelings sometimes are not enough for a person who cannot handle things about you from your past, or maybe cannot deal with your family members themselves.

If you have serious issues to address, find a good therapist and begin working on healing and coming to terms with those issues. This will help you to move forward. It is only fair to your future spouse and children that you are seeking help and are committed to working on the ways you are damaged.

Above all things, experiencing the grace of God through living the sacramental life can raise you above any brokenness and render you capable of being a good spouse and parent. Finding a suitable partner includes finding someone who is gentle and understanding about your past and is willing to love you and accept you as you are.

As you date, share your past with each other and spend time with each other's family. You do not want the past to have any power to disrupt your future together.

Develop Your Character

A person's character refers to their principles and moral standards and how they behave as a result. It's not just what someone believes but what someone does. What you do shows your character. It is the ability to choose what is right, ethical, and good apart from the moral standards of society.

The standards for character among citizens in today's society have sadly been lowered. What was once unacceptable behavior is now accepted and tolerated, or even encouraged. This makes it harder to find quality individuals you can trust for every aspect of life, from doing business to making friends.

For those who are dating, being of good character plays a significant role in finding love. It is amazing how many singles of questionable character believe they can attract a beautiful person with great character and morals. They never ask themselves the key question,

"Would I date someone like me?" If you hope to attract a person of good character, you have to become one yourself.

Good character is expressed by human virtues such as kindness, prudence, generosity, a solid work ethic, politeness, mutual respect, and trust. Without good character, the grace of God cannot be efficacious. Grace builds on nature, not the other way around. Grace cannot be lived without the presence of human virtue. By nature, humans can develop human virtues that make one a good person without any formal worship of God or practice of an organized religion.

A man who keeps his word is a man who is trustworthy. Therefore, a woman can safely trust him when he vows to love her for a lifetime. It is unwise to marry a man who has proven himself to be untrustworthy.

A woman who shows patience, understanding, and attention to people who are difficult to deal with is a kind woman. Therefore, a man can safely believe she will show kindness to him when he is difficult at times in their marriage. It is unwise to marry a woman who has an intolerance and impatience for difficult people.

These are the kind of things that really matter to someone who wants true love, who wants to make a wise choice regarding marriage. Rediscover what it means to be a gentleman or a lady, and then become that person of good character. You will be amazed at the quality of people who will begin to be attracted to you.

Personality Plus

Your personality is the least changeable thing about you. We are born with our personalities, and they are pretty much fully developed by the time we are seven years old, so there is not much you can do about your personality other than learn to accept it and control it.

We all have personality traits, and these traits play a major role in determining who we should marry. Personality clashes are typically hard on relationships; therefore, it is important to be yourself while you date so the full extent of your personality comes out. Often individuals try to suppress certain aspects of their personality in order to win the affection of someone they are very interested in. That does no one any good.

The best remedy for making sure you understand the full extent of each other's personalities is spending lots of time with each other's friends and family. You might be able to wear a mask and put on an act around the person you are dating, but it's not so easy around family and friends. They know you too well, and they will not let you get away with anything phony.

A word about temperaments. Much has been written on this subject, and many self-help books imply that certain temperaments should never marry each other. There is definitely something profitable in knowing your temperament and how different temperaments interact, but do not get too obsessed about it. Love is a mystery, and there is no science to explain why two people are attracted to each other and decide to marry. We all know at least one couple that baffles us as to what in the world they see in each other.

With love, all things are possible. When two people mutually love each other, there is nothing they can't work through together, even if their temperaments are scientifically proven to be incompatible.

Become aware of any of your personality traits that make developing a lasting, loving relationship difficult. Do not insist that the other person accept you for who you are; the things that you can change or tone down about your personality should be worked on. It's good for you, and it's good for the people you date. Just be sincere about it.

Come to terms with whatever you cannot change or are determined not to change, and look for someone out there who will accept these things because they accept all of you. You just never know. There is always reason to hope there is at least one person out there who will.

Keep the Past in the Past

Your past relationships are in the past. Never bring someone you dated in the past into your present relationship. The person you are dating is not that person. Do not project the negative things you may have experienced onto the person you are seeing now. It is not fair, and it does no good.

If you feel any bitterness, anger, prolonged sadness, or any other emotion or pain that is acutely on the surface of your heart and mind, do yourself and your future dates a favor and take a break from dating for a while. You need time to heal. Get help if you need to. Do whatever it takes to find a way to move forward in peace with a positive attitude.

Every person you date provides an opportunity to learn more about yourself, more about others, and more about dating. Accept each relationship as a learning experience. In the past you may have had your heart broken, but you have to move forward. You might very well have been spared being with the wrong person. There are all kinds of ways to look at it, but the reality is that person is your past, not your future.

Past relationships have a way of making us feel like we have failed, or that love will never happen again for us. You invest time in someone, and you invest your heart. Each failed relationship tempts you to decide you cannot take that kind of risk again. That is a very real feeling, and it is natural to feel that way. But you have to find a way to risk again because love is a risk. And the risk is worth it. There is no other way to find love than to take great risks.

You have not failed; you have succeeded. You have taken a step toward marriage and toward fulfilling your vocation. Everyone who risks is a success, even in seeming failure. It is those who do not take risks and avoid relationships, for whatever reason, who have failed.

Keep the past relationships in the past. Take what you have learned and apply it to your next relationship. Be positive and hopeful in your present relationship. And never compare your current date with past ones. Compare experiences, but not individuals. There is no comparison.

Drop the Drama

We all have a flair for the dramatic. We can easily make too much of something, and then we find that something was not as bad as we thought when all is said and done. We also like the attention we get when we dramatize a situation.

This is okay once in a while. But what if your flair for the dramatic comes in larger and more frequent doses? What if you believe that normal everyday life is one dramatic happening after another? What if you find uneventful days to be boring, causing you to go stir-crazy? This might make you a candidate for being a drama lover.

There are some people who just cannot stand an ordinary, dull existence. They enjoy drama in their life, whether it's through constant activity or by creating problems that could be avoided. Their lives always seem to be chaotic. They are attracted to drama, and they attract drama to themselves. Somehow it finds them. These individuals require drama in their life. They cannot sit still or accept when things are going well for too long, so they find a way to create drama that causes unrest and emotionally trying situations. This is troublesome for the person dating a drama lover who just wants things to be peaceful, normal, and stress-free.

Though life has its ups and downs, it is still typically drama-free for ordinary people. You deal with life as it comes. For most of us, life can be as manageable as we choose it to be, even when much of it is out of our control. At the very least, you can control how *you* approach life. And the best approach is to steer clear of unnecessary drama.

The drama lover is dramatic. Therefore, the drama starts within the person. We say sometimes that a person is overdramatizing a situation. By this we mean it is being exaggerated. That is fundamentally the basis of the drama lover. The person has an exaggerated reality, therefore, their approach to life is exaggerated. Their interior life is chaotic; therefore, their exterior life becomes chaotic. Normal things that should just be dealt with are dramatized. They make something out of nothing.

Female drama lovers are commonly known as *drama queens*. A drama queen is melodramatic; she exaggerates, craves attention, and even lies about what happened in order to get more attention or manipulate the situation (often actually believing the lie is the truth). Men can be just as melodramatic; you just don't often hear them referred to as *drama kings*. This kind of male simply gets labeled a nut.

Perhaps you are a drama lover. If you are, be honest, recognize it, and work on it, because bringing drama to a relationship can be very traumatic and draining for the person you date or marry. There are many levels to being a drama lover. You must determine to what extent you love or seek drama in your life and work at becoming as drama-free as possible not only for your own well-being, but also for the sake of your future spouse.

Accept Your Flaws and Imperfections

We are all flawed and imperfect. We all have habits and ways about us that are peculiar and quirky. We all have habits and mannerisms that are irritating, annoying, and even unattractive.

These things do not render us unfit for marriage. Anyone looking for someone flawless and perfect is not only deceiving themselves, but also fundamentally mistaken about what it means to fall in love. Our flaws and imperfections are part of what make each of us unique, and it serves all dating persons well to embrace these aspects of the other person and love them. When you finally marry, you will find that those very peculiarities are endearing and contribute to why you love your spouse. In fact, those who cannot embrace what is imperfect in another are not likely to find love and get married. They are waiting for someone who does not exist, and as a result, they miss out on loving a unique individual. Accepting another person's faults for a lifetime also helps us grow in virtue and holiness.

Having said this, it is wise to take inventory of your own imperfections, habits, and idiosyncrasies. At the very least, you will be aware of them as those you date experience and react to them. Having a good sense of humor helps a great deal. We all need to be able to laugh at ourselves and not take ourselves too seriously. What is imperfect about you is what makes you human and real, and you do not want to assume that this means there is something terrible or unlovable about you.

However, as you begin to know yourself better and take inventory of your imperfections, consider which flaws could be less noticeable or intrusive or possibly overcome or removed completely. As you take inventory, make some observations. Ask yourself these questions: How do these imperfections, habits, and quirks affect my dating success? Can I really hold every person to the "this is me, take it or leave it" mantra, or does it make more sense to consider addressing things that seem to have the same negative affect consistently?

There are things that are unique about you that are just part of who you are. But there are also many more things that you have acquired along the way for one reason or another that can definitely be tamed or stopped.

It is alarming how often an individual believes another person is the wrong person because of flaws and imperfections, when that person is good, kind, and would definitely make a good partner in marriage. Even a very flawed person can have the capacity to offer their life as a gift to another in marriage and make his or her spouse happy, if that person is accepted, flaws and all.

If you struggle to get past what is imperfect about those you date, focus on becoming aware of your own imperfections. This will invoke the humility to realize you should be flattered and honored that this person is interested in you, and you will be more willing to accept the negatives along with the positives.

Do not let your flaws cause you to shy away from being open to marriage. Your flaws are the path to sanctity within marriage; they afford spouses untold opportunities to live with patience, tolerance, and charity toward each other. And I guarantee you there are more flaws you do not even know about yet that will not show up until you are married. Let's face it, it's hard to live with another person. Marriage means having to put up with a spouse and possibly children. But then, your spouse and your children will also have to put up with you. Daily living together exposes your flaws and imperfections and then demands that you work on yourself in order to live your vocation in the best way possible.

We prove love primarily by enduring and growing through the difficulties. The pleasing things make it easy. What is unpleasant makes us saints if we handle them well. We need God's grace, and we need a good sense of humor. But what many do not realize is that we are called to love the flaws and imperfections of our loved ones, and even find them endearing. Endearment encapsulates that person's uniqueness. And it should be their uniqueness you love, excluding nothing but accepting and welcoming all.

CHAPTER NINE

B e c o m e Flexible

THE EASE AND SMOOTHNESS OF how a relationship is going can make a dating couple believe they have found *the one*. They always have a good time. They never quarrel. They see eye to eye on everything. They are perfect together.

But what happens when unexpected things occur? I often tell people that they need to take a long road trip so they get to see all sides of this so-called perfect person. One's true colors emerge during the strenuous circumstances of a long road trip. It is good for couples to see these colors, in order to see how each copes with the unexpected.

Change: Expect the Unexpected

Challenging circumstances and disappointments are a normal (and guaranteed) part of any relationship. If you want to enjoy a relationship of love and happiness, you have to accept that things are not going to go as planned or as you anticipated. Your life together will be filled with lots of unforeseen events. To live life is to encounter the unexpected.

If you cannot cope well with the unexpected, you might have a problem with change. More specifically, it might be that you become easily upset if things do not go as you expect. Change is a given when it comes to marital love. Whenever you live a relationship with another human being, there will be change. Therefore, you have to learn to be flexible. As each person changes during marriage, you make adjustments, and you learn the art of compromise. You might have to change your attitude about life. You cannot demand that your spouse stays the same forever, or reverts to the way things were. It is okay to talk about things so you can help each other make any necessary adjustments. But your attitude toward change should be a positive one, or you will find yourself resenting unexpected, and even unwelcome, changes.

Only God Himself is unchangeable. All creation changes. It is wise to accept that there will be change, and that change is good and natural. To be blunt, those who find change difficult are probably not good candidates for marriage. Do you get upset or take it personally when a friend does something you do not like or goes in a direction you did not expect? Perhaps marriage is not for you until you can do what is necessary to become a person that accepts change.

People who cannot handle the unexpected should consider not pursuing marriage if they are unwilling or unable to change. A relationship of love is a mutual exchange of persons. If you cannot handle who that person is, that does not necessarily mean that they are not the right person. They might actually be the most suitable partner for you, considering you need to change for the better. Love cannot be a one-way street where one person dominates all aspects of life due to their immovability when it comes to how things must be. That is not love, nor is it a healthy relationship.

Everything that happens can be a positive experience if we have the right attitude and disposition. Even things that are legitimate problems that need to be discussed and resolved can be positives because they fashion us into better people, and they help us become the saints we are called to be. If you must have things a certain way, or your peace is disrupted, you are not on the road to sanctity. Marriage to another person is beneficial to reconditioning us to be flexible.

As you approach dating, you don't want to set your sights on finding someone who makes your life easy. You want to find someone who makes it easier to get through the challenges, the struggles, the disappointments, and the unexpected together, as one. I would argue that you use even more caution if you want to marry someone you have never fought with, or if you have not confirmed your own ability to successfully get past negative things caused by this person you think you love. It is good to have worked together through a problem or two in order to test flexibility.

Choosing a marriage partner wisely has a lot to do with knowing that you are capable of handling change. Accept that life is full of the unexpected, and it is the call of true love to cope with these unexpected circumstances and disappointments. This is a major way we help those we love feel relaxed and safe with us and feel the freedom to be themselves.

Keep Your Sense of Humor
One of the best safeguards for dealing with the unexpected in a relationship is having a good, healthy sense of humor.

Very often, we are attracted to someone who makes us laugh. This is a wonderful quality to discover because it is very important to find someone you can laugh with through life. Not laugh *at* life, but *through* life...together. Life is difficult, and it can be full of uncertainty and suffering. The demands of family life, especially when you are raising children, can make you feel overwhelmed. You need each other not only for support and encouragement, but to help you laugh. Without someone you can laugh with, you risk carrying a heavy load that is unbearable and works against your sanity. Laughter is truly medicinal.

However, there is much more to having a sense of humor than just laughter. We do not want to be with someone who never takes life seriously and jokes about everything. There is a place for laughter, but there is also a time to be serious. There is a balance; however, we should never take things (or ourselves) too seriously.

Even when we need to be serious about what is going on, taking things too seriously puts an undo amount of importance on your entire life. And taking yourself too seriously puts an undo amount of importance on your role in the matter or how something affects you personally. Not being able to see past your own expectations means that you are easily thrown off course. The person on the receiving end of this response cannot help but feel they have done something wrong.

Of course, we all take ourselves too seriously at times. There are moments when we become inflexible and cannot seem to adjust to a situation. As a result we get upset or defensive or express some other negative reaction. We allow our feelings or our pride to be wounded. It is a reaction that says, "This should not be happening to me, because I deserve better."

And therein is the humor. We take ourselves so seriously that we actually believe we deserve better, deserve to not have the negative experience, and deserve to not be mistreated. *Deserve?* Now *that* is funny!

Despite our inherent human dignity that says all people deserve to be treated with respect, we are all fundamentally sinners deserving only death and permanent separation from God. Because of God's mercy and kindness, we are reconciled to Him through grace, and we can live in friendship with God both in this life and forever in Heaven. Starting from this basic reality, you can form a sense of gratitude regarding everything that happens during your life.

It must make God chuckle whenever He comes across one of His children who is pitching a fit about a situation He has allowed for the good of that child, but who feels he or she does not deserve it.

Unexpected things happen. Terrible things happen. Surprising things happen. Joyful things happen. Sometimes nothing happens. However life happens, the ability to see through things and not get stuck at the surface helps us to keep perspective.

If the person you are dating has a good sense of humor, you probably notice that they take change and the unexpected in stride. They are not easily discouraged. They are optimistic. They do not let disruption or inconvenience get to them. They can laugh at themselves and make light of the situation. They have the perspective that things are really not that bad. In a word, they are not attached to what *must* be. They go with the flow. They are flexible. This is the nature of good humor.

The inability to cope with the unexpected can make matters worse, which puts undue stress on a relationship, regardless of whether the problem is directly or indirectly associated with the couple. Anytime one person gets disturbed and upset about something, the other person is affected, and the overall relationship suffers. What if your partner might be a little late, but you like to be on time? What if you were really looking forward to doing something and the other person does not feel like it? Building a relationship is about adjusting to the situation when it is called for. So many petty things turn into major issues simply because one person's plans and will must dominate. Far too often, two people dating are ready to give up on the relationship because some difficult circumstances arise, which becomes the excuse to call it quits. This lack of flexibility is a sign that someone might not have good sense of humor.

A typical argument might begin this way: "I'm not even going to talk to you about this anymore because I know I can't change your mind." If you really *know* you cannot change someone's mind, then it is up to you to find peace about it within yourself. Find that peace, accept what you cannot change, and move on. The finding of peace, acceptance, and the ability to just move on is also a sign of a good sense of humor.

How we handle and deal with the unexpected reveals a lot about who we are and where we are in our spiritual life. The most humorous thing about life on earth is that it will end. Seeing through this, we know there is life after death, so making the most of our time here on earth in preparation for eternity is wise. A good sense of humor helps you detach from life in this world so you do not take it too seriously, because any day you might be called into eternity.

Seek Compatibility

Have you ever seen those couples that just seem so perfect together it almost makes you sick? You could say that they are compatible with each other. In this sense, compatibility is a congruence of interests. These individuals have similarities that make it very easy to be together. Another term for "compatible" is "well-suited." The Scriptures call this being "evenly yoked" (see 2 Corinthians 6:14).

There is nothing wrong with seeking someone with whom you share common interests. Hopefully, you have your priorities straight and seek a commonality in your faith; hopefully, you both desire to get to heaven and want to share the path towards it.

Why wouldn't you want to be with someone with whom you are well-suited? Having mutual interests makes for a more pleasurable relationship and provides a strong foundation for love. We have a very romantic notion of couples who are so alike couples with this congruence of interests make marriage look easy.

I read a lot of marriage and relationship books, and the subject of compatibility comes up often. One I read recently concluded that a marriage can legitimately be over if incompatibility issues are discovered along the way. It is true that many divorces are due to incompatibility. But this way of thinking implies that if a couple stops having mutual similarities and interests at some point, they are no longer compatible enough to remain together.

I think it's wonderful to have a congruence of interests and similarities. However, this is not the original meaning of the word *compatibility*, which comes from the following Latin roots:

- *Com* means "with."
- *Pati* comes from the Latin verb *patior* or *patiri*, which means "to suffer; to endure." We get the word *patience* from this Latin verb. The word *passion* in the context of Jesus's suffering comes from *patior* as well. Other key Latin roots are *patiens* and *patientia*, both meaning patience, endurance, and suffering.
- *Ability* or *able* means "capacity" or "capable."

Therefore, technically the true meaning of *compatibility* is "the capacity to suffer with, tolerate, or endure another person." In the context of marriage, compatibility is connected to the vow to love one another through sickness and health, for better and for worse. It is the bearing of one another for the sake of the other. It is to endure unpleasant, challenging, or painful times, as well as traits and behaviors, and to do so with patience and acceptance.

No spouse is perfect, and each one is certainly capable of causing pain and problems within the marriage. Two people can be similar in every way, but they will still annoy or hurt each other at times. Additionally, one or both could change so much that it causes the other hardship to have to adjust and accept what they do not like.

The decision to marry should not be based solely on how much you both get along. It is much more important to know if you are truly compatible, if both of you have the capacity to patiently endure and suffer with one another. If not, then you must decide whether or not you can become compatible.

Suppose your spouse loves football. You, on the other hand, cannot stand football, and as your spouse is talking about football, inside you cringe, or you have a temptation to say something negative. What do you do? Well, you could tell your spouse how you feel straight out. If you do, how would it sound? Or you could keep your feelings to yourself and allow your spouse to enjoy football, accepting that it is something you do not share. You could just smile and be supportive and accommodating, or you could learn something about football in order to share in your spouse's interest.

True love demands that you at least joyfully tolerate your loved one's interests. In fact, the test of your own character and where you are on the road to sanctity is primarily in these moments of having to endure and suffer through something your spouse enjoys but you do not. A fundamental, practical purpose of marriage in God's plan for us is to purify our souls through these moments where we must bear with our spouse, allowing this to fashion us into saints. Did you ever think of it this way?

What if your spouse wants to talk about something you've heard a hundred times before, and you don't really want to waste time listening to it again? This is another occasion to show your compatibility, your willingness to endure the other. When you do this out of love, you endure it joyfully, not begrudgingly.

We say a person is *unbearable* sometimes. These moments are perhaps a good time to go on a retreat or at least go out for a ride in the car to take a break and collect yourself. Better to do that than to blow up at your spouse when you should have shown a more loving endurance.

One thing is for certain. We are called as Christians to bear with one another. "Bear with one another" is another way of saying "be compatible." We are all capable of suffering patiently through difficult times with another person. It might not be fun, and it might feel downright awful, but God's grace given to us as Christians assures us that we can accomplish patient endurance. If we do not, it is to our own detriment, and we have wasted an opportunity to develop good character and deepen our spiritual life. Moments of patient endurance and tolerance move us one step closer to heaven.

Too often, good relationships are destroyed (sometimes very slowly over time) because one or both individuals behave selfishly and uncharitably toward each other by refusing to share the other's interests. An abusive level is reached when one person not only does not want to endure it, but also seeks to make the other person feel bad about what they enjoy and might be trying to share, thus breaking their spirit. This kind of behavior causes serious damage to relationships, because these acts hurt both persons simultaneously.

It would serve all of us well to stop thinking of love only when both persons have common interests and similarities that make the feelings of love ever present. Marriage is much more about enduring and bearing each other patiently. True love bears all things patiently, kindly, and honestly. Therefore, through our dating experiences we should define success as endurance and tolerance, not just good feelings and pleasure.

Are you a compatible person? Are you capable of patiently enduring another person when you don't feel like listening to what that person wants to share or doing what they want to do? Are you capable of allowing another person to grow into the person they are meant to be, even if it means some personal suffering for you? Can you tolerate certain things that bother you?

If you can answer yes, you can be compatible with anyone you choose, because it is you who has to be ready to love when it is hardest to do so. Two people that share this kind of compatibility are able to have a happy and lasting marriage, even when affection might diminish or die, or when you no longer have similar interests.

If the answer is no, however, then you must develop compatibility. Learn to be a person who is able to endure, tolerate, and suffer along with a future spouse. Become someone who can handle and deal with the unexpected.

Trust in God and Be Out of Control

In Psalm 81, God lets us know He is anxious for us to allow Him to take care of us. If only we would keep faith and trust in Him! He reminds us of all He has done and what He is capable of. "Open wide your mouth and I will fill it" (Psalm 81:10).

Sadly, most of us are control freaks. We believe intellectually that we should trust in God in all things, but we are inclined to trust in our own ability to control our situations. We lose sight of God and allow fear to cloud our reason. We are too impatient to wait on the Lord, and too stubborn to turn to Him first before we take our shot at controlling things.

Many single Catholics struggle with knowing they should trust in God and leave the matter of their vocation to marriage in His capable hands, despairing that it will never happen or acting destructively on their own behalf. We want someone to come along right now because we think we are ready now. This is the classic childish attitude of wanting what we want when we want it.

If we are being honest, we would admit that our faith and trust in God is weak, while the faith we have in ourselves is much stronger. It seems much more logical to trust in our own ability to make things happen to affect our bottom line for a future marriage.

The result is one failed relationship after another, as well as a good deal of interior hardship that makes it difficult to maintain a perfect peace and joy. We fail in our relationships and we struggle with unrest and loneliness in between relationships because we do not trust in God. He has no choice but to leave us to our own designs.

Our own designs—what are they? They are the multiplicity of thoughts and actions that stem from the primary inclinations of our fallen human nature, that of desiring to follow our own will. We are stubborn about our will. We like our will. We trust ourselves and our own ability to plan. We lack the humility to act appropriately in our lives in accordance with God's will, which is the only way to effectively prepare for and live marital love.

In a word, we are inflexible. We are firmly invested in our own will, and having trust in anyone else, even God, is too risky. After all, who better to solve my problems than me?

The flexible person, however, understands that although we have a definite part to play in God's plan, much of everyday life is affected by others and very much out of our control. The flexible person also acknowledges that God is ultimately in complete control, and they have a childlike surrender to God in all things.

This complete reliance on God is an acknowledgment of Him as Father. To be out of control allows the Father to be in control. With God as Father, you can be flexible about the unexpected things of life and trust that your Father will bring about good from them. Taking control of your life, on the other hand, means that you decide you do not need God as Father. He, in turn, respects that decision and pulls His Fatherly hand back. It is much better to seek God's will with great flexibility.

It is no easy thing to stare in the face of God's will and say yes. Original sin has instilled a ferocious pride in each of us that does not want to relinquish control. The practice of considering God as Father works to diminish the control freak in us, making us more and more flexible. It is no coincidence that Jesus taught us to appeal to God as Father, most obviously via the Lord's Prayer, which we should say daily and with thoughtful consideration.

Be careful of living a double standard, saying you trust in God and saying the Lord's Prayer, yet living in such a way that excludes God from your decisions and activities, or else appealing to Him only when it is convenient or after first trying it your way and failing.

Are you going through the motions of living the faith, but still consistently living in ways you know contradict the teachings of the Church? Or perhaps you want to meet a quality Catholic in hopes of marriage, yet you do not want to change in ways that would attract such a person. Maybe you are quick to blame and find fault with the people God brings into your life, yet you do not examine yourself or ask Jesus to reveal your faults. Maybe you desire a Catholic marriage but approach it for selfish reasons.

It is the ultimate double standard to say we love God and trust Him to take care of the things, and then to be stubborn about letting go. We need a single standard in our lives, one that relies on God for all things. We also have to be able to trust others, especially the person we eventually marry. Otherwise, we are looking to control the relationship.

Being flexible with those you date allows you to practice giving up control and allows you to learn to trust. Without trust, marital love cannot survive. So it makes sense to practice now and learn to surrender having everything your own way. True love has no double standard, and it has only one face: the face of Christ among us.

Do not resist God in favor of your own designs. Trust Him. Let Him take total control. You will have perfect peace and happiness, and you will become very attractive to the opposite sex. With this kind of trustful surrender, whether marriage happens or not is inconsequential because you are already in sync with God. But this does take humility. Pray for it daily, and pray Psalm 81. God wants to take complete care of you. Become flexible as life comes at you, and open wide your mouth so that God can fill it.

CHAPTER TEN

B e c o m e **Practical**

HAVE YOU REALLY THOUGHT ABOUT what married life demands? Are you committed to becoming a person who is ready and able to be married? Or are you dating irresponsibly, only concerned with the romantic and affectionate aspects of falling in love?

Being practical is imperative, especially in the realm of dating and marriage. Real marital love is first and foremost practical and with social purpose. God needs marriages for the greatest glorification we human beings can give Him, which is children. Children help form families that establish sound societies in this world, as well as populate Heaven. This is the most basic purpose for marriage. Added to this are all the practical ways men and women as partners help each other. The stability of marital love helps individuals live in peace and purpose.

To Settle or Not to Settle

Everyone wants to find a person who makes them feel the kind of love we hear in classic love songs. We all want fireworks and strong feelings of attraction and romance.

Wouldn't it be wonderful if everyone who is called to marriage found this kind of love? Maybe, but maybe not. Many people never experience this level of romantic love, and they remain single because they do not want to settle for anything less.

What is it that makes them feel they are settling, and why is this such a bad thing? Many people feel that they cannot be happy or really be in love if there are no fireworks, no hearts beating fast, no strong passionate desire, etc. While it is certainly wonderful to experience all these things, it is impractical to think you are entitled to it and misguided to believe all married couples enjoy this kind of romantic love.

It would be a mistake to settle for someone you do not love and accept, marrying them only because of the utility they provide. One example might be a woman who wants to bear children before it is too late, or a man who wants someone to cook for him. These are practical things, but if there is no real love for the person involved, then the person you are marrying is used as an object.

On the other hand, it is okay to settle on someone if "settling" means that you choose to love the person first and foremost and that person chooses to love you. I know this is not a popular idea, but it is possible to have a successful marriage even without strong attraction and passionate feelings of love. You can choose to give yourself to a wonderful person and live out a practical partnership within marriage. The love is not driven or inspired by the passions, but by the quality of the person and the reverence for the vocation you both are called to.

Do not misunderstand me: Love is definitely a requirement, or it is wrong to get married. But the kind of love portrayed in love songs and movies is not the basis of the requirement. Friendship that mutually desires the good of another is love, and a good marriage can begin with and be sustained by a mutual commitment to give love to each other.

It is very possible to have a lasting love for someone because of their kindness, out of respect for them, or maybe because of how you are around them. A love that begins from these attractions can grow into deep feelings of desire along the way.

We have to believe that God can bring two quality people together capable of giving to each other and thus fulfilling the marriage vocation even though they do not have the romantic love people insist is required. And we have to be open to becoming the type of person who can love at this very practical level.

All kinds of good reasons can bring two sincere people together in marriage. No one should be made to feel like they are merely settling if they want to marry a person with whom they do not experience romantic sparks with, but whom they respect, trust, and enjoy being with.

Married life is demanding, and without a practical approach to marriage, it cannot be lived out properly. I do not care how religious you are or what a good person you are. There are plenty of good people who are impractical people and thus risky choices for marriage.

It is impractical, for example, for a man to be fixated on finding a stunningly gorgeous woman without concern for her domestic interests or capabilities. It is also impractical for a woman to focus on finding a financially well-to-do man without concern for his leadership qualities or temperament.

A practical approach to marriage is the best place to start. While you are dating, it is important to consider the practical aspects of marriage, or else you allow yourself to put too much stock in the mesmerizing elements of romantic love to the point of declaring that nothing else matters because you are in love. Hogwash! Many other things matter!

All that is required is mutual agreement. Both individuals must feel the same. If you put an undue emphasis on romantic feelings, considering them a must have, it might keep you from making a practical decision in marriage.

Living out one's marriage vows is not about what one *gets*, but what one *becomes*. Your marriage is meant to help you become a better person and a saint. A marriage to a good person goes a long way toward helping you get rid of selfishness. This is very practical. As a result, another person is loved, and children are brought into the world who also are loved and bound for heaven. Anyone can have a good, happy, loving marriage with or without the fireworks, as long as there is a mutual acceptance of what they have and a commitment to that reality. It might not be the ideal, but then again, what married couple is living the ideal? How many divorces are between two glamorous, charming, delightful, outgoing, good-looking people who were passionately attracted to one another at one time? Why does this happen? What else do they want? They want what they are not willing to become themselves.

Capable of Marriage

Living the vocation of marriage is not about the *ideal*, it is about the *practical*.

Marriage is a practical sacrament and institution. It requires two people who not only want to be married, but who are capable of fulfilling the demands of marriage. Too often, people go into marriage full of love and good intentions, but without the personal skills to fulfill their roles. As you live marriage, practically speaking, you should mature and realize what you are to do, learning the skills along the way as you interact and live with each other and your children.

Marriage is on-the-job training. You cannot be perfectly prepared for it. But you can be totally committed to it and open to becoming what is necessary along the way through the experience. This is the practical approach. If feelings are the benchmark for how the marriage is going, then trouble awaits. You have to understand that feelings of love may or may not be there, but your commitment to one another remains regardless.

The *capacity* for marriage must be taken into account; however, when it comes to any couple, this is only practical. What good is it to let romance dominate when the priorities of married life are not so romantic, and they demand so much more than romance can sustain? It is definitely a fact that there are people who desire marriage that just should not get married, whether because of a temporary or permanent lack of capacity.

The reality is that great numbers of marriages are ending in divorce, and many times it is because the couples who entered into them should not have ventured into marriage to begin with. Often one or both spouses were actually unfit for marriage, and thus incapable of living out that which they vowed.

The sad truth is that a person's incapacity for marriage is not easily recognizable before the wedding. It is usually discovered after the fact. However, you can begin to discover how practical a person is just by being aware of all that marriage demands, understanding the roles of a married man and woman, and talking to each other about what is involved.

If a person you are dating does turn out to be impractical about marriage, and only interested in focusing primarily on the romance the two of you have, you will have to navigate things towards becoming practical people before you get as far as marriage. If this is not possible, it might be time to end the relationship.

A Practical Vocation

If the impractical tendencies are discovered after the marriage, then every effort must be made to turn things around. Too many marriages end in divorce due to selfishness, a lack of forgiveness, and a lack of endurance through difficult times that could have been salvaged through time, effort, and God's assistance. To leave your spouse, for example, simply because you want somebody else, don't have feelings of love anymore, or because things aren't turning out the way you expected is inexcusable.

As long as two people can be harmonious and not hurt each other, and as long as they can both perform all of their marital requirements and duties, they can make it through by God's grace.

Again, this is not a popular view of marriage, but that is because people do not make being practical about marriage a priority. Two people have a natural right to be married, but not necessarily a right to always feel pleasure in marriage. There is nothing about the promises of marriage or the teachings of the Church about what marriage is that indicates pleasurable feelings of love must always be in place. Marriage is mutually helping each other, being open to life, educating and raising children, permanence, fidelity, and commitment to each other in sickness or health, wealth or poverty, good or bad times.

Two people make a commitment to be each other's partner and work together for each other's good for a lifetime. You might suffer, but you will not have to worry about being abandoned. You might not feel the romance, but you will be loved because your spouse is always there, doing his or her part. It is security. And joy and happiness can be found in that security.

Bring Out the Best in Each Other

Too many ill-willed spouses have fashioned a prison for the person they married, a prison that person did not deserve nor should be expected to endure. Many times the offending spouse has no idea of the harm he or she has caused their mate. This is very tragic, but it happens. And it happens because one spouse is incapable of fulfilling what they entered into.

It is impractical to stifle the person you marry. It is more practical for both spouses to be themselves and bring out the best in each other, not one spouse being dominated by the other one to the point of becoming unable to function. Responsible employers do not do this to their workforce, but on the contrary, they attempt to provide their employees with an enjoyable working environment, one that makes them more productive and loyal to the company. Marriage should be the same.

It's never too late, however. For couples who come to a realization that they are unfit for marriage, there is still hope. With counseling, a sincere effort, a commitment to change, and especially with God's grace, they can turn things around for themselves and become equipped with the tools necessary to be good spouses.

Sadly, some individuals are deeply invested in the way they are and will never be willing or able to change. They truly are incapable of marital love. These singles can live a very productive, fulfilling life in their work and among loved ones.

How can you be practical and avoid marrying someone unfit? This is not easy, and often couples do not discover this until after they get married and start living together. That is why it is very important to use your time well during the dating process and engagement period. You must strive to radically uproot all the harmful things that distract you from making a practical choice, like being sidetracked by the way someone looks or what they do for a living.

Be practical and learn as much as you can about a potential spouse's background and upbringing. Observe the person's relationships with their family members and friends (especially their parents), ask lots of questions that pertain to the past and future, and do your best to share and learn each other's dreams, goals, and interests. If anything seems like a red flag, bring it up and see if you can reach a satisfactory resolution. Do not allow feelings of love to distract or blind you from what is important. Pray together, and make sure you know that Jesus Christ is the most important person in each of your lives.

But do not make this into an interrogation; do not be confrontational. You are trying to grow in love and depth with each other, not impose and insist. Allow the relationship to be natural while you both stay practical about the ability of your relationship to be lived out in marriage.

For those capable of a sacramental marriage, making the lifelong commitment in marriage is liberty and freedom at its best. Love is exchanged and lived out, even through difficult times. It is not an imprisonment forced upon you. It is more like Christ's sacrifice of love, voluntarily laying down your life for the other.

Remember, you, a sinner, are dating and marrying a sinner. Everyone fails. Expect that there will be failures and be prepared for them. How we respond to failures and grow from them is what matters, especially when it comes to forgiveness. No one is perfect, least of all you. Consider yourself a worse sinner.

Called to a Mutual Exchange of Love

It is a popular notion that the love between a man and a woman should be unconditional. This is a very romantic notion but not at all practical. Who wouldn't want to be loved unconditionally in marriage? But the fact is love *is* conditional. Both individuals love each other; the condition for the other being a better person is you being a better person, and vice versa. No one can sustain an entire lifetime of marriage carrying the entire load unconditionally.

Though we are called by Jesus to love all human beings, having an impractical expectation about the love between a man and woman sends the wrong message. Do we really want to be in this kind of marriage? Do we really find it appealing that we should love the other despite anything they might say or do?

It certainly would be great if someone loved us unconditionally so that we were assured of receiving love without us having to return it, wouldn't it? Or would it?

Actually, it would not be great at all. What kind of person would you be if you thought you were free from loving your spouse while your spouse loves you completely? A pathetic person, I'd say. What you are actually saying is that your spouse can carry the load of love when you are in an unlovable period of time. You must be able to return the favor.

Unconditional love calls us to love our enemies and do good to those who persecute us. It is a call to forgive, to be a peacemaker, and to pray for everyone. It is unconditional because it is a deliberate act of the will in the name of God, having nothing to do with how the other person responds.

Though we are called to pray for an enemy, we are not expected to live with them. It is one thing to have to put up with a boss who is mean. Because you do not have to live with him, you can find a way to tolerate the situation. The Lord has given all who are baptized the mission to love unconditionally. This is *not*, however, the mission of married couples to each other.

Marital love is a mutual love, a mutual giving of persons to each other. It is consciously choosing another person. It is a love that accepts love's failings. It grows from these falls on the condition that there is a desire and an effort to improve. The love is sustained despite ongoing failures because being with that person is more of a positive than a negative.

Who would go into marriage if they knew that their spouse was going to stop loving them, and they would be stuck loving a person who no longer loves them? No one! That is the worst situation imaginable. To have to love someone who does not love you in return and have it not affect you so you can always sustain that love is unrealistic, to say the least. A successful, fulfilling Christian marriage where both persons grow as individuals happens only on the condition that the love is mutually exchanged.

No marriage is perfect, meaning both persons are mutually exchanging love at all times. Moments of failure are certain. As one spouse fails, the other spouse can help the fallen one up through forgiveness and understanding. The couple starts again and moves forward, maintaining at the core that intention and commitment to mutually give of themselves and reinvest in the marriage because of the vows they made.

As you date, be able to recognize a person's capability to have a mutual love exchange. If someone seems too self-centered or controlling or is not supportive of your interests, pause and consider if this is what you want.

It is very possible to get so caught up in the wonderful things about the person you are dating that you are blind to very important signs that the person will not be able to sustain the mutual love required in marriage. The individual might be a very lovable person, but are you willing to love this person for a lifetime despite their unloving tendencies? Perhaps you are. I'll say it again: The person you marry must be more of a positive so that any negative is bearable. In other words, you love them despite their faults.

To love someone despite their faults is also a very romantic notion. However, Christian marriage is too important a call to be entered into loosely or foolishly. You have a moral obligation to determine the difference between a fault and an impediment to mutual love. Your love for another person must transcend the romance of emotions and feelings and be grounded in the practical world of actions that build up the person God calls them to be, and it must service the immediate family and extended community.

Ask yourself during the dating process: Do I see both of us displaying a capability and desire to serve and accept each other for who we are, while being able to extend forgiveness when we fail?

Preserve One Another's Dignity

The dating process is the opportunity to practice this mutual love exchange, and this is very practical. You cannot start the official ball game if you do not see any potential during practice. Again, marriage is on-the-job training, and as you live marital love, you will grow better and better at it. However, you cannot expect this kind of mutual love to happen within marriage if one or both of you are not qualified.

It is a terrible thing when one of the partners becomes unlovable and makes the other person feel trapped or puts them in a position of suffering. It is at these unfortunate times that the one who has to carry the load of the marriage must love the other unconditionally. This is an incredibly difficult thing to accomplish; it requires a union with God and cooperation with divine grace. Many people are not spiritually developed enough to endure times when unconditional love is called for. It makes sense that the relationship dies. Whether they divorce or not is irrelevant. The death of love is, in and of itself, a tragedy of marriage. This internal death not only affects marriage and family life, but it causes the loss of one this individual's person-hood. He or she becomes a shell of a person merely going through the motions of daily life.

This does not mean you have to put up with every type of treat-ment. Abuse, for example, whether verbal, physical, mental, or psychological, threatens to harm the spouse being abused. A person in a marriage that threatens to harm them does not have to take it and in many instances has an obligation not to allow it.

This is not the dignity of marriage intended by God. We must do all we can to ensure that our marriages give glory to God through mutual love exchanged, as well as the children that the couple co-creates with God.

Though most marriages have hardships, they can all have the dignity marriage requires. This starts with both persons acknowledging each other's personal dignity. Without dignity, there is mistreatment and abuse, which is an offense to marriage.

Love all people unconditionally, but grow in mutual love with your spouse. You need each other to give true love to each other. Do not expect each of you to carry the load of loving indefinitely. That is not the call of marital love, and it is very impractical toward successful marriage.

Real Romance

Candy, flowers, dinner dates, and many other expressions of romantic love have their place. But the real romance is committing to love each other daily, putting each other first, and being good friends. Nothing says "I love you" like being a person your spouse can count on, who is always there. Sharing this kind of love in marriage is priceless.

CHAPTER ELEVEN

A Meditation on the Crucifix for Singles

"We become what we love and who we love shapes what we become. If we love things, we become a thing. If we love nothing, we become nothing. Imitation is not a literal mimicking of Christ, rather it means becoming the image of the beloved, an image disclosed through transformation. This means we are to become vessels of God's compassionate love for others."

—*attributed to St. Clare of Assisi*

As you have read, you are destined to become a resurrected and glorious son or daughter of God, enjoying Him forever in heaven. Your time on earth is a time of becoming that saint through the sufferings and failures of this life, as well as the restoration by grace and the virtuous life you live.

Fundamental to becoming a resurrected son or daughter is first becoming crucified with the Lord Jesus Christ in this gift of life you have been given.

For Catholics, the crucifix is essential for living out our daily lives. The crucifix is the symbol of Christ's ultimate act of love for us. The crucifix depicts Jesus nailed to the cross and dying for our sins. We hang crucifixes on the walls of our homes and wear crucifixes around our necks so that we will be visibly reminded of Jesus's love for us and the price He paid for our redemption.

For those who desire a deeper relationship with Jesus Christ, the crucifix also serves as an ideal focus of meditation. Archbishop Fulton J. Sheen said that the summary of all our sins can be found on the crucifix. It is, therefore, the perfect way to examine our consciences.

Examining our consciences while gazing on the crucifix will differ from person to person, depending on our state in life. For unmarried Catholics who are open to marriage, an examination of conscience while meditating on the crucifix should include considerations related to the desire and efforts toward marriage.

Everything Jesus suffered on the cross has a direct correlation to any and every sin possible to commit, and He suffered through His body for them all. The following is an example of an examination of conscience for those who are single, dating, and desiring to be married one day. It is meant to be done while meditating on a crucifix.

The Sacred Head Crowned With Thorns

The sins we commit in our minds

The very mind of God, all His wisdom and knowledge, is mocked when His head is crowned with piercing thorns.

- Do I allow and foster impure thoughts?
- Do I allow myself to harbor ill will toward members of the opposite sex?
- Am I still scarred from past relationships, causing my attitude going into a new relationship to be closed-minded?
- Do I harbor resentment toward those who have hurt me in the past, and do I allow that to affect my current relationship?

- Am I thinking about other things while I am with someone I am dating? Do I think about someone else I would prefer to be with?
- Do I date people I already know I would never marry just to have someone to go on a date with?
- Do I think about inappropriate sexual things while on a date?
- Do I try to think of ways to get the person I am dating to have sex with me?

The Hands Nailed to the Wood of the Cross

The sins we commit with our hands

Hands that gently touched others and were used for healing and performing miracles are nailed to wood like common parchment.

- Have I tried to touch a person I am dating inappropriately or impurely?
- Have I ever physically hit someone I am dating?
- Have I avoided doing things for the person I am dating, such as cooking for them, or doing works of charity?
- Do I masturbate while looking at images of the opposite sex or while thinking about the person I am dating?
- Do I write dishonest information about myself or send uncharitable messages on dating websites?

The Feet Nailed to the Wood of the Cross

The sins we commit with our feet

The feet that took Jesus all over Judea so that so many people could experience the Incarnate Word among us and come to believe are now made stationary with one nail through both feet.

- Have I used the gift of walking to visit illicit places where I do not belong?

- Do I make the extra effort to get to places I should go that benefit others and myself, or am I too lazy?
- Do I busy myself too much going here and there, thus depriving myself of necessary rest?
- Do I avoid going out on dates because I would rather indulge in my own selfish interests?
- Do I procrastinate going to places or into environments that would offer me a chance to meet a quality person of the opposite sex?
- Would I rather stay home and wait for God to bring my future spouse to my front door, or do I keep my feet moving to do my part so God can do His part?
- Do I walk with people who will enhance me as a person, or do I prefer those who get me into trouble or lead me away from God?

The Body of Christ, Stripped of Its Garments

The sins of the flesh we commit

As if He is not humiliated enough from the scourging and the carrying of His cross, Jesus's body is fully exposed as His clothes are removed.

- Have I exposed myself inappropriately to a person I am dating?
- Have I tried to remove my date's clothing in an attempt to engage in premarital sex?
- Do I show too much of my body publicly?
- Am I mindful that chastity is as much in the mind as in the flesh or in my manner of dressing?
- Have I become numb, indifferent, or conditioned to nudity or exposed flesh so that I am no longer affected by it or do not even realize I should be affected by it?

- Do I strip others of their dignity through my callous or cruel words and behavior?
- Do I take pride in clothing my body and take care of how I dress, or do I consider it everyone else's problem if they do not like the way I dress?
- Have I stripped myself of all that would distract me from God, or have I at least made a lifelong commitment to daily work on all that distracts me from God?

The Sacred Heart Pierced With a Lance

The sins we commit in our hearts

Blood and water bursts from Jesus's side after his Sacred Heart is pierced, showering the crowds with the fullest extent of His love and cleansing those who would be splashed with the graces of mercy.

- Am I protective of the heart of the person I am dating?
- Am I careful not to break the heart of the person I am dating through insensitivity or selfishness?
- Do I see the heart of the person I date as something to win by making that person feel safe?
- Am I too quick to feel love for someone I am dating, making that person, as well as myself, vulnerable to heartbreak?
- Is my heart too guarded to allow the person I am dating to get to know me and develop love for me?
- Am I patient and gentle, and do I create a homey atmosphere that allows my date to feel safe enough to share openly with me?
- Am I a good friend, or am I hard to get to know and too quick to cut someone off when things go wrong?
- Is my heart forgiving with a motive for bringing about peace, or do I prefer unrest and discord because of a hardened heart?
- Do I lust after members of the opposite sex in my heart?

- Does my heart desire things that are incompatible with true love and marriage?
- Do I allow my heart to be attached to someone whom I could never be married to?
- Is my heart pure, allowing me to see God in everyone?
- Is my heart open to change in myself?
- Am I flexible with the things that happen in life, or is my heart sad when things do not go as planned?
- Is my heart in the right place, or do I have ulterior motives in the things I do or say concerning someone I am dating?
- Are my priorities straight when it comes to what and who I love?
- Do I let my heart rule my decisions instead of consulting my mind and determining what is most prudent and for the best despite my feelings?
- Do I love God with all my heart and desire to keep His commandments, or do I prefer my own will?
- Am I too attached to someone to the point that I willingly desire to please them before God?

The Outstretched Arms
The sins we commit by being unwelcoming

Jesus's arms are pulled out as far as they can go, as if to show us that God loves us that much. Who among us can ever extend our arms out so fully and say we love anyone that much?

- Am I a welcoming person? Do I make people feel comfortable?
- Are my arms always outstretched and open to comfort those who need it?
- Do I offer my arms to give hugs?
- Do I offer the person I am dating chaste hugs to show my affection and care?

- Is my attitude in life to smile and open my arms to receive, or do I always look miserable and reserved and keep my arms at my sides? Am I standoffish?
- Can everyone find mercy with me, or am I easily offended and make people feel guilty or inferior?

Christ Suffers in Silence

The sins we commit with our lips and our speech

Amidst the chaos of the crowd shouting at Jesus to save Himself and come down from the cross, He silently endures, speaking very little, and only when necessary.

- Am I quick to talk and slow to listen?
- Do I complain about every little thing when I should endure them silently and patiently?
- Do I speak without thinking or without considering the other person?
- Do I enjoy badmouthing the opposite sex and gossiping about bad dates?
- Do I remain silent and accept annoying things on a date, or do I insist on making comments?
- Do I look for positive things to say about the person I am dating?
- Do I say "I'm sorry" when I have said or done something wrong?
- Do I say things that will help resolve problems with the person I am dating, or do I remain silent and allow things to get worse, while waiting for the other to make things right?
- Do I say the words "I love you" without backing it up with my actions?
- Do I speak kindly and with self-control, or do I raise my voice or shout to make my points?
- Do I monopolize the conversation or talk only about myself?

- Do I not talk enough and keep to myself too much, making others uncomfortable trying to find things to talk about?
- Am I abusive in my conversations with the person I am dating, making them feel bad, hurting their feelings, or trying to manipulate them?
- Do I have a sincere desire to use the gift of speech to build up others and not tear them down?

Christ's Eyes Are Impaired by Blood and Are Closing From His Approaching Death

The sins we commit with our eyes

The blood from Jesus's pierced head drips into his eyes, which now have only a distorted vision of the world.

- Do I look appropriately at the opposite sex?
- Do I realize that my eyes are the windows to my soul and everything I look at affects me?
- Do I lack the will power to guard my eyes from those things I know are wrong?
- Do I look at pornography?
- Do I watch too much television or too many movies?
- Do I overindulge in visual entertainment or watching the news?
- Do I feel compelled to see the things I allow myself to see?
- Do I make eye contact with the person I am dating, or do I look away a lot?
- Do I make my date feel uncomfortable by looking at him or her inappropriately?
- Do I look around at other members of the opposite sex while I am out with the person I am dating?
- Am I wise and prudent about what I watch and read?

- Do I criticize the person I am dating when I observe what they do?
- Do I observe the needs of the person I am dating, or am I to self-absorbed to notice?
- Do I pay close attention to the things that are unique about the person I am dating and his or her interests so I can really get to know them?
- Do I do things for my date that show I have been paying attention to who they are?

Christ's Blood Poured Out From Every Part of His Body

The sins we commit from holding back giving our life to others

With the last of the life of Jesus extinguishing from His body, His ultimate decision to lay down His life for us proves the truth of what it means to love.

- Am I the kind of person who will do anything for anyone without counting the costs?
- Do I desire to pour out my life for the person I will eventually marry?
- Do I practice total self-giving with the people that are in my life?
- Am I selfish? Do I prefer to always have what I want and do what I want before considering the needs of others?
- Do I have my own agenda about how events should unfold?
- Am I impatient with the person I date, not giving the relationship a chance to develop?
- Am I only looking for someone who will serve me and please me in every way, or am I seeking someone whom I can serve and give my entire self to?
- Do I have the capability of loving someone with all their faults and imperfections, or am I only willing to consider marriage if I

know the other person will always make me happy and never hurt me?

- Do I see myself giving as lovingly in marriage as Jesus gave Himself in love for me on the cross?
- Am I willing to choose a suitable partner and move forward with a loving marriage, or am I always making excuses for why I should not give myself completely to someone God has put into my life?

These are but a few questions to consider. As you pray before the crucifix, allow the Holy Spirit to inspire you with further details of your life. It is all there on the cross for you to discover. The grace and enlightenment is available to aid you in what you are to become.

NOTES

1. Pope St. Gregory the Great, *Forty Gospel Homilies* (Piscataway, N.J.: Gorgias, 2009).
2. St. Augustine, *City of God* (Peabody, Mass.: Hendrickson, 2009), section XIX.13.